THE NON-TORAH

Exposing the Mythology of Divine Oral Torah

International Alliance of Messianic
Congregations and Synagogues (IAMCS)

Cover designed by Cover Designer

An official publication of the International Alliance of Messianic Congregations and Synagogues (IAMCS)
Visit our website at: www.iamcs.org

Printed in the United States of America

First Printing: April, 2019
IAMCS

ISBN – 9781092390378

CONTENTS

Chapter One: Origins

Preamble:

We, as the leadership of the Messianic Jewish Alliance of America (MJAA) and the International Alliance of Messianic Congregations and Synagogues (IAMCS), do from time to time find it necessary to express our voice on certain matters which may arise, which potentially have a bearing on the clarity of the messianic Jewish witness and testimony that we are called to express to the world. We set forth this official publication in recognition of our calling and duty from the Lord to vouchsafe certain principles of biblical doctrine which we consider to be fundamental and sacred.

Naturally, while there are countless erroneous teachings out there in the world, we would scarcely feel any need, let alone desire, to publish books or papers responding to or commenting upon them. However, we do find it necessary if it is the kind of an issue that touches upon Messianic Judaism in such a way that it has potential to cause confusion as to certain basic tenets and precepts of our faith in Messiah. In that instance, we feel there is a need and a duty on our part to speak to the error in question.

This is one of those instances. The reason for the official IAMCS publication of this book is to address a teaching which comes from within the realm of orthodox rabbinic Judaism. Specifically, it is the teaching which claims that there is an oral Torah given by God to Moses at Sinai. There are variations on that teaching, but it is generally something that is associated with orthodox rabbinic Judaism.

However, there are also those wolves among the sheep who come into the messianic Jewish fold, with an agenda to import the mythology of oral Torah into Messianic Judaism. This gives rise to a unique concern for us as messianic Jewish leaders.

Consequently, we feel compelled to address the erroneous nature of the claim of divine oral Torah. In so doing, we intend additionally to address its origins, how it developed historically in rabbinic Judaism, how it has negatively impacted generations of Jewish people right up to today, and how some have sought to import the teaching into the messianic Jewish movement.

The Issue:

In the simplest terms, the issue is this: Whether, in addition to the written Scriptures, there is such a thing as a divine oral Torah given by God to man.

Preliminary Discussion:

As to that issue, we in the MJAA/IAMCS maintain unequivocally and without exception that the answer is "no." There is a man-made oral tradition which developed historically among the Jewish people, of which some is good, some is not so good, and some is just plain wrong. However, the Jewish oral tradition is not the Word of God.

Whatever value one may place upon the oral teachings and practices of rabbinic Judaism, it must be clear that it is not the Word of God. The written Scriptures of the Tanakh (Old Testament) and B'rit Chadasha (New Testament) are the authoritative Word of God. They are unparalleled. There is nothing else on the level of reliability nor trustworthiness other than the written Scriptures.

There is no oral Torah that was given by God. Not to Moses. Not to the Patriarchs. Not to anyone. Any claim that there is another "Torah" of divine nature, given orally, but not written down, is a false claim. Such a mythical Torah is not a Torah, but a non-Torah. Hence, the title for this book.

Origins of Rabbinic Judaism:

Rabbinic Judaism is an historical development which is not the original biblical faith of the Jewish people that is found in the Tanakh. For one thing, Rabbinic Judaism is founded and constructed upon the belief, found nowhere in the Scriptures, that an oral Torah was given directly by God to Moses at Sinai. That belief is fundamental in rabbinic Judaism.

Unlike former days, when Israel was led by Davidic kings or by Judges and Prophets of the Lord, and maintained an independent Temple and Priesthood, Rabbinic Judaism developed in a political vacuum wherein Jews were trying to adapt to life under the rulership of foreign nations. Rabbinic Judaism gained traction in the immediate aftermath of the destruction of the Second Temple. Upon the pretext of being the heirs of a divinely-transmitted oral law, rabbinic Jewish leadership created and adopted countless man-made laws not found in the Bible and portrayed them as having been given by God to Moses at Sinai.

Many rabbinic-made laws were based on sound wisdom and put forth for good purposes. Many others were based on legendary accounts, far-fetched stories, and were not enacted for good purpose. In either case, the rabbis who created the oral tradition, together with the claim that it was given directly by God, used the mythology of oral Torah in order gain the confidence of the people and to lift themselves up as religious leaders over them.

The Rabbis eventually recorded their oral teaching in written format in the Talmud, followed by later writings as well. Two versions of the Talmud emerged, one drafted in northern Israel (*Talmud Yerushalmi* or Jerusalem Talmud), the other drafted in Babylon (*Talmud Bavli* or Babylonian Talmud).

The drafting of the Talmud created a more concrete body of rabbinic teaching and law. The writing of the Talmud, which is considered at least equal in authority to the written Scriptures, greatly advanced the cause of rabbinic Judaism to create a religion governed not by the Tanakh, but by the teachings of the Rabbis.

The Pharisaic Connection:

Rabbinic Judaism is rooted in Pharisaic Judaism that existed at the time of Yeshua. The Pharisaic connection is clearly seen in the New Testament, as the early stage of rabbinic Judaism was happening within the same historical context as Messianic Judaism of the First Century. The Pharisees are mentioned often in the New Testament. It is indeed an ironic twist of history that the New Testament is probably the best resource for discovering the origins of rabbinic Judaism.

The Pharisees existed along with other sects of Judaism at that time. But it was the Pharisees who developed the mythology of oral Torah. When the Second Temple fell in the year 70 CE, Pharisaic Judaism filled the void. Rabbinic Judaism soon came into full bloom. It replaced the Temple system as the spiritual center of Jewish life with a Judaism that was essentially Pharisaic and based in the oral law mythology.

The destruction of the Second Temple happened just about forty years after Yeshua preached in it and was rejected by the *Sanhedrin* or Jewish high court. Except for the many tens of thousands of Jews who believed that Yeshua is the Messiah, the destruction of the Temple, and consequent exile, left our Jewish people otherwise as sheep without a Shepherd. This situation was prophesied by the prophet Jeremiah, but with the promise of redemption of Israel in the end-days:

> *"Woe to the shepherds who are destroying and scattering the sheep of My pasture!" It is a declaration of* ADONAI.
>
> *Therefore, thus says* ADONAI, *the God of Israel, about the shepherds who feed My people: "You have scattered My flock, driven them away, and have not taken care of them. I will soon visit on you the evil of your deeds." It is a declaration of* ADONAI.
>
> *"I will gather the remnant of My flock out of all the countries where I have driven them, and will bring them back to their folds, and they will be fruitful and multiply. I will raise up shepherds over them who will feed them. They will no longer be afraid or dismayed, nor will any be missing," It is a declaration of* ADONAI.*"*[1]

The Myth of Two Torahs:

Belief in a divine oral Torah is the cornerstone of the house built by post-Temple rabbinic Judaism. The mythology, along with the power and influence of the post-Temple-era rabbinic establishment, was greatly advanced by the drafting of the Talmud.

---

[1] Jer. 23:1-5. All Scripture references are taken from the Tree of Life Version, unless otherwise indicated.

The basic idea is that the Torah was given by God to Moses at Sinai in two parts: "Torah *shebichtav*" (Written Torah), and "Torah *sheba'al peh*," (Oral Torah). The Rabbis claim to possess the oral Torah, which makes them the authority on the Word of God. This authority, of course, includes the right to decide who the Messiah is.

There definitely is an oral tradition of the Jews which goes back to ancient days. After all, God gave His Word, the written Bible, to Israel. Consequently, the spiritual leadership of the Jewish people has been tasked with the unique responsibility to rightly interpret and apply to life the written Scriptures given by God to Israel. From this task, teachings and practices developed naturally among the Jews, which were conveyed orally through the generations.

However, the claim that Jewish oral tradition is actually a divine revelation given by God to man *in addition to* the written Scriptures, is a matter found nowhere in Scripture. It is a claim initially created by Pharisaic rabbinic Judaism, then propagated by those who rose to power as religious authorities among the Jewish people in the era following the fall of the second Temple and consequent diaspora.

Independent of the claims put forth by the rabbinic community itself, which the rabbis drafted into the Talmud, no evidence exists anywhere of an oral Torah given by God. The oral law mythology, therefore, is self-perpetuating, as it depends on the system itself to continue the myth. To those who embrace it, any other movement among Jewish people would automatically be considered unacceptable to them.[2]

Rabbinic Judaism was not originally a part of the ancient, biblical culture of the Jewish people. The early foundations of what later became "rabbinic Judaism," began with the Pharisees, who emerged after the victory of the Maccabean revolt and rededication of the Temple in 164 BCE. Because the Hasmonean rulers lacked the legitimacy of the Davidic dynasty, a political vacuum formed. This enabled "bourgeois" religious scholars and scribes to rise to power and influence. The Pharisees arose in opposition to the Sadducees, the ruling elite, who were closely connected to the Temple Priesthood.

This period in Jewish history is also called the period of "*Zugot*" (pairs). During that time period, the

---

[2] Even among rabbinic Judaism itself, there are deep factions in which the orthodox see any non-orthodox Judaism, as somehow not really a "Judaism." In Oct. 2018, for example, when a horrific mass shooting occurred at a conservative synagogue in Pittsburgh, the chief Ashkenazi Rabbi of Israel, David Lau refused to call the venue a "synagogue." He instead referred to it as a "place with a profound Jewish flavor." See:
https://forward.com/fast-forward/412889/israel-chief-rabbi-wont-say-pittsburgh-shooting-synagogue-orthodox/

Sanhedrin was led by pairs of leaders, five in all, which ended with Hillel and Shammai in the year 30 CE.

One of the great points of contention between the two parties of the Pharisees and Sadducees was that the Sadducees insisted upon the authority of written Scripture alone, while the Pharisees developed many religious traditions not found in Scripture and insisted upon the divine authority of their traditions. The Jewish historian Josephus, in *the Antiquities of the Jews*, describes this tension between Pharisees and Sadducees over the issue of oral law:

> *"What I would now explain is this, that the Pharisees have delivered to the people a great many observances by succession from their fathers, which are not written in the law of Moses; and for that reason it is that the Sadducees reject them, and say that we are to esteem those observances to be obligatory which are in the written word, but are not to observe what are derived from the tradition of our forefathers. And concerning these things it is that great disputes and differences have arisen among them. While the Sadducees are able to persuade none but the rich; and have not the populace obsequious to them: but the Pharisees have the multitude on their side. ..."*[3]

---

[3] Josephus, Ant.XIII,X,6., written in approximately 93 CE.

Probably due to their wealth and elite status, the Sadducees were not liked nor trusted by the Jewish masses. Moreover, when the Temple fell, their place and purpose was essentially eliminated.

Thus, the opportunity for the establishment Pharisaic Judaism was greatly advanced by the fall of the second Temple in 70 CE. The fall of the Temple resulted, for the most part, in the disappearance of the Sadducees from the scene of Jewish history. Meanwhile, the Pharisaic religious sect filled the void, and morphed into what became known as "rabbinic Judaism" in the post-second Temple era.

To Yavneh and Beyond:

Birthplace of modern Rabbinic Judaism

The chaos which followed the Temple's destruction opened the door for the Pharisees to seize the reins of spiritual leadership once held by Priests and Levites. Thus, following the fall of the Temple and destruction of Jerusalem in 70 CE, Rabbi Yochanan Ben Zakkai, a Pharisee, moved the Sanhedrin to Yavneh.

Most historians see Yavneh as the birthplace of modern rabbinic Judaism. Prior to Yavneh, the Temple was the center of religious identity for Jews. Jewish life was deeply connected to the Temple. With the Temple gone, the process began in Yavneh for adapting and creating a Judaism that could exist without a central Temple. What was created in Yavneh became the new standard of religious identity and practice for Jews.

With the Temple system gone, and blood atonement no longer possible, the rabbinic community in Yavneh scrambled to try and come up with a new approach to Jewish religious life. After all, if atonement is such an important precept of the Scriptures, how then can it be carried out without the Temple? Messianic Jews already saw God's answer, provided by the blood of His Son Yeshua. However, as messianic Jews embraced biblical, atonement-based Judaism, the rabbinic community at Yavneh came up with another idea: *Teshuva*, *tefila* and *tzedakah* (Repentance, prayer, and charity).

- To do more than Required
- Acts of Loving Kindness

From now on, thanks to the idea that came out of Yavneh, atonement no longer was connected to the shedding of the blood of an innocent life. Even though the principle of the Torah was clear, that there is no atonement without the shedding of blood.[4] As the Torah explicitly says:

---

4 Heb. 9:22.

"For the life of the creature is in the blood, and I have given it to you on the altar to make atonement for your lives—for it is the blood that makes atonement because of the life." (Lev. 17:11)."

This new theology—*teshuva, tefila, tzedakah*—that came out of Yavneh was a change in the law. How can this happen? How can God's law be changed? This is the operation of so-called oral Torah. It's a never-ending stream of non-Torah that is supposed to be actual Torah. It is law-making by men based on the pretext that the laws they make are the Word of God. And in many cases, their laws override the written law found in Scripture. Since God gave (allegedly) the Rabbis the power to say what is or is not the law of God, they can dispense with a basic Bible principle like atonement, and come up with a new thing – repentance, prayer, and charity – to replace atonement.

It was a clever way for rabbinic Judaism to continue without the Temple, and to maintain its rejection of the crucified Messiah. After all, the Messiah must take David's throne and reign as Prince. He is not to lay down His life for our sins. Whatever Isaiah 53 might say to the contrary doesn't matter. So long as the Rabbis say it doesn't speak of a crucified Messiah, then so be it. That's how oral Torah works. An elite body of men are vested with authority to tell everyone else what the Word of God is.

This step which occurred at Yavneh most radically and drastically changed Jewish life for centuries, right up to today. As such, rabbinic Judaism is not an atonement-based faith, but a religion inundated with extra-biblical rules which are to be thoroughly learned and obeyed as the means of meriting one's righteousness. These rules are created, defined, and regulated by the Rabbis.

This is why, for example, there are voluminous discussions and tedious rules found in the Talmud and later rabbinic writings, instructing on how Jewish life ought to be lived. Judaism thus became bogged down with legalities, not related to Scripture, involving the superfluous and extraneous details of how one ought to observe Shabbat and festivals, how to pray, what to wear, what to say, when to say it, etc., etc.

Comparatively, in biblical Judaism, atonement is an absolute essential. All three of the practices offered by the Rabbis in place of atonement—*teshuva, tefila, tzedakah*—are indeed important, but they can't replace the need for atonement through the shedding of blood. What came out of Yavneh was not the Judaism of the biblical time. It was a fundamentally different Judaism. And at the root of this fundamental change was the idea that the Rabbis had the power and authority to change the Word of God. Because, according to oral law mythology, the oral law *is* the Word of God.

The Judaism of the Early Messianic Jews:

It is no historical coincidence, that at the same moment in history in which the Temple fell and the Pharisees rose to power, there was a growing movement of Jews both in the land and in the diaspora, proclaiming that our Jewish brother, Yeshua, is the Messiah. According to these Jews, the man who was condemned by the Sanhedrin as a blasphemer and who was handed over to the Romans for crucifixion, was actually the Son of God. Not only was there a growing movement of Jews proclaiming Yeshua to be the Savior of Israel as prophesied in the Tanakh, but masses of Gentiles throughout the Roman Empire also were joining themselves in one faith with these messianic Jews.

Clearly, in the immediate aftermath of Jewish history following the destruction of the second Temple,

Jewish religious leaders could not ignore the fact that an increasing mass of humanity, both in the land and in the diaspora, was proclaiming a Jew from Galilee to be the Messiah. Without a doubt, as the agenda of rabbinic Judaism took its form, it was in large part a response to the Yeshua-movement.

That is not to say, however, that the early messianic Jews were in some way revolting against all things Jewish. They indeed were at odds with the rabbinic community over the issue of the identity of Messiah; not, however, over the issue of Jewish identity.

Quite to the contrary of the fictional version of history which strips the early Jewish believers of all Jewishness, as was popularized by the Church and embraced historically by the Christian world, the early Jewish believers embraced their Jewishness. While the messianic Jews of the First Century clearly ran into conflict with those Jewish religious authorities of their time who rejected Yeshua and His teachings, nevertheless, the messianic Jews did not cast off Judaism. They were not in rebellion against the Temple Priesthood nor against Judaism as a whole. They did not in any way disavow biblical Jewish practices, nor their own Jewish identity, nor their Jewish cultural heritage.

While Church history would have the world see early Jewish believers as disavowing both their Jewishness and Judaism in its entirety, that is simply not accurate. Instead, the first messianic Jews were coming together with Gentile believers in a lifestyle of faith and practice which both parties saw as true biblical Judaism. They saw themselves as witnesses, called to reveal the identity of Messiah to the Jew first, and, also to the Gentile.[5]

In the beginning of the post-Temple era of the First and Second Centuries CE, the Jewish nation was struggling to maintain its identity. In stark contrast to what came forth out of Yavneh, Messianic Judaism of that era was a faith community in which Jews embraced and strengthened Jewish identity as believers in Yeshua. At the same time, the faith they maintained was inclusive and welcoming of the Gentiles. And, unlike what developed later in Christianity, non-Jews at first saw their calling to serve alongside of Jewish believers. Together, they embraced Israel and prioritized a Jewish expression of messianic faith, seeing it as the scriptural imperative for all believers in Messiah. This is essentially the same vision unto which we adhere in Messianic Judaism today.

---

[5] Rom. 1:16.

In spite of the messianic Jewish identification with Israel and biblically Jewish expression of faith, rabbinic Judaism rejected messianic Jews. However, a Pharisee named Sha'ul, who was raised at the feet of the great Talmudic scholar Gamaliel, became one of them.[6] Also many from the Kohanim and Pharisees and observant Jews throughout the land joined the community of messianic Jews, and were proclaiming that Messiah had come in the form of the man from Galilee.[7] And masses of Gentiles were also turning to the biblical faith brought to them by messianic Jews.

As Jews came to faith in Yeshua, Rabbinic Judaism felt threatened, and thus saw a need to put the messianic Jews out of Jewish community life. Yeshua described this reaction in advance, saying:

"They will throw you out of the synagogues. Yes, an hour is coming when whoever kills you will think he is offering service to God."[8]

Nothing could stop the spread of that gospel fire which was being ignited by messianic Jews both in the land and in the diaspora. The Yeshua-movement of that era, just as today, relied upon the Scriptures as the basis

---

[6] Acts 22:3, Philippians 3:5.
[7] Acts 6:7, John 12:42, Acts 21:20.
[8] John 16:2.

of faith for both Jewish and non-Jewish believers in Yeshua:

"Everything written concerning Me in the Torah of Moses and the Prophets and the Psalms must be fulfilled. Then He opened their minds to understand the Scriptures." [9]

Accordingly, the oral law mythology was also utilized as a way of responding to the *"minim"* or so-called Jewish "heretics," which were the Jews who believed in Yeshua, referring to the written Scriptures of the Tanakh as authority for their belief.

The rabbinic establishment was stuck with the difficult task of declaring that Yeshua is not the Messiah, even though the written Scriptures do clearly show that Yeshua IS the Messiah. Therefore, the Tanakh, according to the Rabbis, was not to stand on its own authority. There was another "Torah," allegedly given by God to Moses and passed down to the rabbinic community, without which the written Scriptures could be neither interpreted nor applied – or so the claim developed.

For about five hundred years following the Yeshua-movement, rabbinic Judaism created the

---

[9] Luke 24:44,45.

Talmud. But in another more profound sense, rabbinic Judaism was *created by* the Talmud. For once it was written, it became, for all practical purposes, the "Bible" of the post-Temple Jewish religion.

In the same era when the Messiah came to the land of Israel and raised up tens of thousands of Jews who followed Him, Pharisaic Rabbis rose to power as the new spiritual masters of the Jewish people. All the while, they have maintained this false shepherding of our Jewish people for hundreds of years through the pretext that they were the heirs of a supposed oral law given by God.

The heart of messianic Jews is to bless our Jewish people with the good news of salvation. God has an irrevocable plan for the salvation of Israel.[10] The ancient fable of a divine oral Torah has been an obstruction to God's plan for the salvation and restoration of Israel. Thankfully, as God opens Jewish eyes to the truth, this is the day of its hasty removal. The mythological veil is being lifted, and Jewish people are coming to see the Truth as found in the teaching of the Holy Scriptures. Baruch HaShem.

---

[10] Rom. 11:25,26.

Halakha – Tradition vs. ~~Law~~

Jewish religious law is generally referred to as *"halakha."* Halakha literally means "the way of walking." The idea of halakha makes good sense when approached simply as a traditional way to live out the Word of God. But the problem arises when the halakha itself is viewed as the Word of God.

Traditionally, halakha developed organically as an attempt to apply the Scriptures. For example, how to celebrate Shabbat, how to perform a circumcision, how to present the first fruits of the harvest, how to afflict one's soul on Yom Kippur. The effort to interpret and apply Scripture to life naturally results in a tradition for doing it. It is only natural that the Jews, unto whom the Bible was given, would have a body of tradition, outside of the Bible, in order to help us live the life which God appointed in the Bible.

But in rabbinic Judaism, there is a plethora of halakha that is either far beyond what Scripture intends and/or has nothing to do with Scripture at all. That is where the whole matter of halakha becomes rather sticky. It inevitably raises certain questions about studying and/or observing halakha. For example: Are we doing this because God says or because the Rabbis say? Is there a difference?

In rabbinic Judaism, where the oral tradition of the Rabbis is treated as "Torah," there really is no difference. After all, halakha in rabbinic Judaism is considered not just orally transmitted cultural tradition, but, rather, as part of *Torah sheba'al peh* or oral Torah, which is believed to have been given by God to Moses at Sinai along with the written Torah.

Biblically, the responsibility to interpret and apply the Scriptures to Jewish life was given mainly to the Priests and Levites.[11] The Pharisaic sect was not vested with that authority. But during the 150-200 years before Yeshua came, the political situation enabled the Pharisees to gain favor with the people and rise to a level of prominence.

By Yeshua's time the doctrine and tradition of the Pharisees had grown quite strong. It was referred to as "the tradition of the elders"[12] by the writers of the New Testament. That tradition was the key reason for much of the conflict with the Yeshua-movement of that time. Yeshua did not follow all the customary rules and regulations that they sought to impose. Moreover, among the biblical customs which Yeshua did follow, He didn't necessarily do it in the manner which the prevailing Pharisaic tradition insisted upon.[13]

---

[11] Deut. 33:10: *"They will teach Jacob Your judgments and Israel Your Torah."*

[12] Mat. 15:2, Mark 7:3

While customs and traditions are the natural course of any culture, there is a clear difference between tradition vs. law. Tradition is not necessarily treated as mandatory, in the sense of law. We Jews are a people with a long history, and a rich cultural heritage. We have always had the Scriptures, given by God. And along with that, our traditions are often related to that life which God gave us. But then, along came this thing called "halakha."

Jewish halakha as it was being crafted by the Pharisees, began to be presented in such a way that it was not custom or tradition, but, rather, mandatory religious law. Moreover, halakha often involves hair-splitting issues addressing every conceivable minutiae of life, and oftentimes pertaining to things having nothing to do with either the Temple service nor with anything else in the Tanakh.

As rabbinic halakha emerged in rabbinic Judaism it gave authority to the creators of halakha to declare what is and is not God's word, irrespective of the written Scriptures. Thus, the creation and imposition of religious halakha, was not only a way of regulating religious life, but more importantly, a way of leveraging the power, and increasing the force of the party of those who make the halakha. Which at first case was the

---

[13] See, e.g., Mark 2:23–28 (Picking grain on Shabbat). Mark 3:1–6 (Healing on Shabbat).

Pharisees, and which today is the orthodox rabbinic establishment.

Halakha can be, and usually is, completely unrelated to the Bible. A good example of this from the New Testament addresses the matter of washing hands and cups, of which there is no such requirement in Scripture:

> *"Now the Pharisees and some of the Torah scholars who had come from Jerusalem gathered around Yeshua. And they saw that some of His disciples were eating bread with unclean hands, that is, not washed. (For the Pharisees and all Jewish people do not eat unless they wash their hands up to the elbow, keeping the tradition of the elders. And when they come from the marketplace, they do not eat unless they perform a ritual washing. There are many other traditions they have received and hold, such as the washing of cups, pitchers, copper vessels.) The Pharisees and Torah scholars questioned Yeshua, "Why don't Your disciples walk according to the tradition of the elders? Why do they eat bread with unwashed hands?"*[14]

The New Testament documents how the Pharisees often argued and promoted their man-made religious laws as if equivalent to the Word of God. Yeshua,

---

[14] Mark 7:1-5

however, affirms Scripture as the authority, but denies the authority of the ruling scribes and Pharisees to add or subtract to the written word. Specifically, when harassed, mocked and tested by Pharisees, as Yeshua often was, He never missed an opportunity to rebuke them and make the point that neither He nor His *talmidim* (disciples) were bound to follow their man-made religious system.

The Sadducees, on the other hand, though no friend to Yeshua, had comparatively few encounters with Him. The reason being, the Sadducees did not have a body of oral law which they considered divine. They believed in the authority of the written Scripture only, and maintained a dispute with the Pharisees over their claims of a divine oral law.

While the power of the Pharisees was based in the claim to be the heirs of a *"Torah sheba'al peh"* (Oral Torah), the Sadducees were empowered mainly through their status in the service of the Temple. This placed the Sadducees in unique favor as cohorts with the Romans. Thus, when the Temple fell, the Sadducees as a sect essentially fell with it. They disappeared from future Jewish life. Meanwhile, Pharisaic Judaism, which did not depend upon the Temple, nor upon the written Scriptures, morphed into what we now know as rabbinic Judaism.

The Pharisaic claim to be the "ark–bearers" of an allegedly divine oral law is the reason why they, and not the Sadducees, were constantly clashing with Yeshua. It is that very issue—oral law—which so boldly contradicts the ministry of the Messiah. The controversy over the Pharisaic claim of divine oral law is also the reason why Yeshua frequently made condemnatory remarks to the Pharisees. There are far too many such remarks to list here, but this one, for example, sums up the controversy from the messianic Jewish point of view:

> "But woe to you, Torah scholars and Pharisees, hypocrites! For you shut people out of the kingdom of heaven. For you do not enter yourselves, nor do you let those enter who are trying to go in."[15]

It should be noted that Yeshua did not ever condemn the Jewish people, nor even Judaism. What He condemned was the hypocrisy of the religious leaders, in particular, that of the Pharisees. Everywhere Yeshua went, He preached the Good News of the Kingdom of God. He did not preach or teach rabbinic halakha.

---

[15] Mat. 23:13.

The Gospel Message:

The Gospel message was and still is a drastically different message than the one propagated by rabbinic Judaism. The messianic message is simple and true, and open to all human beings: *"Repent for the kingdom of heaven is at hand!"*[16] That is what Yeshua preached. He preached it with signs and wonders and miracles, and many Jewish people in the land of Israel believed in Him. It was Jewish people who brought the Gospel message to the world to begin with.

However, as for the Pharisaic religious establishment, which survived the exile and the destruction of the Temple, they rejected and opposed the Gospel message. They put the messianic Jews out of the synagogue and community. They put forth the claim that Yeshua was a false prophet—an error which prevails to this day in rabbinic Judaism.

Although Yeshua was recognized as Messiah by a multitude of Jewish people in Israel, the messianic Jewish faith became officially thought of as *not* the "religion" of the Jews. This happened even though the Jewish faith in Yeshua increased rapidly in the First Century CE. Thousands upon thousands of Jews believed in Yeshua, even many who were of the Priestly class:

---

[16] See: Mat. 4:17.

"The Word of God kept on spreading, and the number of disciples in Jerusalem greatly multiplied; even a great number of the kohanim were becoming obedient to the faith."[17]

In spite of the rapid growth of messianic Jews in the First Century CE, as Scripture bears witness, the Good News was opposed by the ruling rabbinical establishment. The pretext for accusations against messianic Jews typically was based on the ground that they were in violation of the law of God. Because for these accusers, "the law of God' did not mean the written Scriptures, but the oral law. We can see this for example in the incident with Stephen:

"Then they secretly instigated men into saying, "We have heard him speaking blasphemous words against Moses and against God!" They also incited the people, the elders, and the Torah scholars; and they rushed at Stephen, seized him, and led him away to the Sanhedrin. They set up false witnesses who said, "This man never stops speaking words against this holy place and the Torah. For we have heard him saying that this

---

[17] Acts 6:7.

*Yeshua ha-Natzrati will destroy this place and **change the customs that Moses handed down to us**.*"[18]

When they accuse him of *"blasphemous words against Moses and against God,"* and of violating *"the customs that Moses handed down to us,"* this is a reference to the alleged oral law that God gave to Moses. Their idea is that Stephen has violated the rabbinic customs, traditions, and *halakha* given by God to Moses at Sinai.

So it is that the Good News message inevitably calls into question the authority and the teaching of the oral tradition of the Pharisees. Sha'ul also was accused concerning the "customs" as if those customs are equivalent to the Word of God:

> *"They have been told about you—that you teach all the Jewish people among the Gentiles to forsake Moses, telling them not to circumcise their children or to walk **according to the customs**.*"[19]

The phrase *"according to the customs"* is likely a reference to rabbinic law which they claim was handed down by God to Moses at Sinai. As Sha'ul and other early messianic Jews saw firsthand, to follow the Scriptures is never enough to satisfy the rabbinic leaders. Because for

---

[18] Acts 6:11-14 (emphasis added).
[19] Acts 21:21 (emphasis added).

TZAK
Righteous acts of loving kindness

them, "God's law" includes not just what Moses wrote down, but also their so-called *Torah sheba'al peh* or oral Torah.

This is why the attempt of Sha'ul to demonstrate that he was a keeper of "the Law"[20] would necessarily fall short and be somehow not enough to convince his accusers. No matter how "observant" Sha'ul may or may not have been, it wouldn't matter. They would go right on finding some pretext for accusing him of violating the law based on rabbinic halakha. That was and still is the real issue for messianic Jews as we relate to our Jewish people as witnesses of the Good News of Messiah.

The message Yeshua preached contradicted the oral law claims of the Pharisees. That often put Him at odds with those leaders who wanted people to think they must learn from the masters of oral law in order to merit righteousness and/or be acceptable for the kingdom of God. Yeshua's message was completely different:

> *"Now is the fullness of time," He said, "and the kingdom of God is near! Turn away from your sins and believe in the Good News!"*[21]

---

[20] Acts 21:21–40.
[21] Mark 1:15.

The claim of Pharisaic Judaism to a divine oral Torah was contrary and antithetical to the simplistic salvation message declared by the Yeshua-movement. Yeshua left no doubt about the fact that this would lead to a final clash. He plainly told His talmidim what would happen on account of the Gospel message:

> *"Then He began to teach them that the Son of Man must suffer many things and be rejected by the elders and ruling kohanim and Torah scholars, and be killed, and after three days rise again."*[22]

Yeshua emphasized that His message of the Kingdom of heaven coming to earth was not a continuation of the Pharisaic system. By its very nature, rabbinic Judaism clashed with the gospel message of Yeshua. This is why seemingly insignificant issues like hand-washing blew up:

> *"As He spoke, a Pharisee asked Yeshua to eat with him, so He entered and sat down. But the Pharisee was surprised when he saw that Yeshua did not do the ritual handwashing before the meal. But the Lord said to him, 'You Pharisees clean the outside of the cup and plate, but inside you are full of greed and wickedness.'"*[23]

---

[22] Mark 8:31.
[23] Luke 11:37-38.

The Talmud:

Rabbinic *halakha* developed over many centuries, but the process was greatly advanced by the drafting of the Talmud. Written into the Talmud is the mythology of divine oral Torah. The drafters of the Talmud wove that into the fabric of Talmud.

The Talmud was written in two parts. First, the Mishna was finalized in about the year 200 CE, due mainly to the efforts of Rabbi Judah HaNasi. In the Mishna, Rabbi Judah recorded the sayings of the Tannaim, which means "repeaters" or "teachers." The Tannaim consisted of about 120 of the leading Rabbis who lived from about the years 10–220 CE.

The second part of the Talmud, the Gemara, was finalized in about 500 CE. The Gemara is mainly composed of the sayings of the "Amoraim," which means "those who say" or "those who speak over the people." The Amoraim were hundreds of leading Rabbis who lived during the period after the Mishna, from about 200-500 CE. The things they said were recorded in the Gemara as clarifying and commenting upon the Mishna.

By reducing the rabbinic oral tradition to writing via the Talmud, this added great force to the claim of rabbinic Judaism that their *halakha* was the Word of

God, given first to Moses at Sinai.[24] On a practical level, the gap left by the lack of a Davidic King or Priesthood in the post-Temple era was filled by the rabbis. But this was accomplished by the creation of the myth that the word of the rabbis is the Word of God.

Messianic Judaism lacks neither High Priest nor Davidic King. We have both in Messiah Yeshua. Rabbinic Judaism has claimed that the Talmud is from heaven. As Yeshua said to the religious authorities who opposed him:

"All too well you reject the commandment of God, that you may keep your tradition.[25]

The Talmud should not be underestimated in its importance nor dismissed outright. What should be summarily dismissed is the claim that Talmud is the Word of God given to Moses at Sinai. The Talmud is a great work in many respects. But those who drafted it, claimed that it is Torah. It is not Torah. It is a non-Torah, created by man.

---

[24] The question of how the revelation of oral Torah to Moses at Sinai was somehow transmitted to future generations, is discussed at length in a later section in this paper.

[25] Mark 7:9.

Rabbinic Influence on Messianic Judaism:

Messianic Jews typically do not reject rabbinic Judaism outright. What we reject is the premise of the rabbinic claim to a divine oral law. As a direct consequence, we reject the authority which the Rabbis have presumed upon themselves to make law as if it is equal to the Word of God. That has resulted, among other things, in the disastrous rabbinic decision which proclaimed that Yeshua is not the Messiah.

Jewish people today are extremely diverse when it comes to matters of religion. However, Messianic Jews are in a totally unique position due to our faith in Yeshua. While diversity of religious belief is commonplace among the Jewish people, it is mainly just Messianic Jews that the rabbinic establishment of today seeks to cast off as apostates.

Nevertheless, we continue to identify with our Jewish people, even though some may not identify with us. We do not completely reject rabbinic Judaism, even though it may reject us. What we do reject are made-up rabbinical teachings which contradict the Scriptures given by God to Israel.

Christian anti-Semitism in Europe did much to complicate the issue of whether it is possible for Jews to believe in Yeshua without betraying one's identity as a

Jew. The long history of anti-Jewish Church doctrine, and Church-sponsored persecution of Jews, all of which culminated in the Holocaust, has served to give credence to the rabbinic claim that the "Messiah" of Christianity is not the Messiah, and that in any case Jews should not believe in him. To that, most messianic Jews would probably agree. Most would respond, "we don't believe in *that* Messiah; but in the Messiah of the Bible." Thankfully, there are many Christians who believe in the biblical Messiah too.

In fact, among Jews, Messianic Jews tend to be the most vocal and outspoken critics of Christian anti-Semitism. As many MJAA/IAMCS publications testify, Messianic Jews often lead the charge against Christian BDS supporters. Theologically, our position papers demonstrate how we oppose all manner of replacement theology. We are generally Zionistic, pro-Israel, promoters of a "One-State Solution," and we are engaged in widespread humanitarian relief to Jews within the State of Israel.

Despite the opposition of rabbinic Judaism toward us both historically and today, nevertheless, Messianic Judaism remains influenced by rabbinic Judaism in a significant way. To some extent, the culture, custom and tradition of rabbinic Judaism can be found in every messianic synagogue worldwide. This is true even though we know that much of it likely originated with Pharisaic Judaism.

When messianic Jews light candles on Shabbat or at Hanukkah; when we march the sefer Torah in a processional and kiss it; when we say the Shema or the Amidah; when we put on a kipa or affix a mezuzah to the doorpost of our homes, etc; we are well-aware that these customs are part of the culture of Jews, preserved and handed down by rabbinic Judaism. Yet, we maintain no delusion that these practices which inhere in Jewish culture were given to us by God at Sinai.

Tradition, culture and religious law made by the rabbis was indeed transmitted generationally. Some of it is good, some not so good. Some of it is outright bad. In any case, it isn't God's word. Accordingly, while Rabbinic tradition is embraced by Messianic Jews, it is with the understanding that tradition is part of the fabric of our Jewish lives. But it is not Torah.

Messianic Jews of the modern era have established that Jews can continue to embrace our Jewish culture and practice our time-honored traditions, without in any way encroaching upon faith in Yeshua. After all, Yeshua Himself and all His first *talmidim* (disciples) were Jews. The people who brought the Good News of Messiah Yeshua to the Gentile world also were Jews. Being Jewish is something that messianic Jews take quite seriously, as did the Jewish Apostles, and the early Jewish *talmidim* of Messiah. To quote the Jewish Apostle of Yeshua, Shimon Kefa:

> *"You are the sons of the prophets and also of the covenant that God cut with your fathers, saying to Abraham, 'In your seed shall all the families of the earth be blessed."*[26]

The modern messianic Jewish movement has proven to the Jewish people and to the world that you can believe in Yeshua and still be Jewish in culture and practice. Messianic Jews pray from a Siddur, read from the Haggadah on Pesach, and have public reading of the *sefer Torah* (Torah scroll). We celebrate communally in Jewish wedding ceremonies, bar or bat-mitzvahs, apples dipped in honey on Rosh HaShana, dress up on Purim, and spin dreydels and give gifts on Hanukkah with a lit menorah in our homes. We do all those things not because they are mandated in Scripture, but because they are part of our Jewish tradition.

There is no conflict with being Jewish culturally and believing that Yeshua is Messiah. The conflict arises only if we endorse and accept the essential premise of rabbinic authority, which is based on a divine transmission of oral law beginning at Sinai. Inevitably,

---

[26] Acts 3:25.

that requires one to accept many things, including the determination that Yeshua is not the Messiah.

We as messianic Jews are respectful and thankful regarding the rich cultural heritage found in rabbinic Judaism. But we are not under that yoke of rabbinic authority, just as our chief Rabbi, Yeshua, being the Son of God, made clear that He was not under it, nor were His followers.

Sha'ul, who came up in the heart of the rabbinic establishment, as a student of the great Talmudic scholar Gamaliel,[27] was appointed by that establishment to be a chief persecutor of the messianic Jews,[28] having them beaten and hauled off to prison and even put to death on account of the gospel. As Sha'ul himself testified:

> *"Even though I was once a blasphemer and a persecutor and a violent man, I was shown mercy because I acted in ignorance and unbelief."*[29]

In the immediate aftermath of Yeshua's resurrection and ascension into heaven, the effort of the rabbinic establishment to persecute and silence the Jewish believers in Yeshua became greatly intensified.

---

[27] See, Acts 5:24, and 22:3.
[28] 1 Cor. 15:9.
[29] 1 Tim. 1:13.

The aim was clear: Silence the community of those Jews who say Yeshua is Messiah, and stop their message from proliferating:

> *"Now Saul was in agreement with Stephen's execution. On that day a great persecution arose against Messiah's community in Jerusalem, and they were all scattered throughout the region of Judea and Samaria, except the emissaries. Some devout men buried Stephen and mourned deeply for him. But Saul was destroying Messiah's community, entering house after house; and dragging off men and women, he was throwing them into prison."*[30]

In today's world, orthodox rabbinic Judaism is still quite hostile toward messianic Jews. The orthodox leaders would like for the Jewish people to continue in the idea that you can't be Jewish and believe in Yeshua. Moreover, they would like to paint messianic Jews as traitors and apostates who seek to proselytize and convince Jews to forsake being Jewish, even to convert to "Christianity." None of this is true, of course, but it is an ongoing conflict that has been happening for nearly two thousand years. With the emergence of the modern

---

[30] Acts 8:1–3.

messianic Jewish revival, the issue has once again come to the forefront of Jewish thought.

To attempt to deny that there is any conflict between messianic Jewish faith and orthodox rabbinic Judaism is a position that flies in the face of reality. The roots of this conflict, replete with all the false accusations made by the rabbis against Messianic Judaism is vividly illustrated in the book of Acts. The simple crux of the conflict with rabbinic Judaism, and the key reason why the religious leadership of the First Century, CE felt the need to persecute messianic Jews, was because messianic Jews did not recognize the authority of rabbinic *halakha* as being of divine nature.

That is not to say that members of the Sanhedrin and/or the extended members of the Priesthood and Pharisaic leadership could not turn and accept Yeshua as Messiah. Many of them in fact did just that. But most did not. And it is a clear point of history, documented by the Bible, that the Jewish religious leadership rejected Yeshua, then went on a rampage to try and stamp out messianic Jewish faith by force.

To be clear, the Jewish people did not reject Yeshua. The Jewish religious establishment did. In so doing, that leadership collaborated with the Romans to have Yeshua crucified, and thereafter to stop the spreading of the message that He was resurrected.

In any case, Yeshua willingly went like a lamb to slaughter, and did what He had come into the world to do.[31] He died once, for the sins of all Mankind, the Father having laid upon Him the iniquity of us all.[32] In this manner, by His wounds, we are healed.[33] Both Jew and non-Jew alike, from every nation, tribe and tongue, whosoever calls upon His name is saved. Meanwhile, the people who believed in Yeshua first were all Jews. It was these Jews who brought messianic faith to the Gentile world.

After Stephen was put to death upon the word of Sha'ul, much persecution arose against the Jewish believers in Yeshua, as he was instructed to continue the effort of the religious leaders to stamp out the fire of Messianic Judaism that was spreading throughout the land:

"Now Saul, still breathing out threats and murder against the Lord's disciples, went to the kohen gadol. He requested letters of introduction from him to the synagogues in Damascus, so that if he found any men or women belonging to the Way, he might bring them as prisoners to Jerusalem."[34]

---

[31] Is. 53:7 – "He was oppressed and He was afflicted, yet He did not open His mouth. Like a lamb led to the slaughter, like a sheep before its shearers is silent, so He did not open His mouth."

[32] Is. 53:6.

[33] Is. 53:5.

Later, on the way to Damascus to carry out these orders, Sha'ul had a divine encounter, the result of which caused Sha'ul himself to become a believer and Apostle of Messiah Yeshua sent to the Gentiles to declare the Good News.[35] Now Sha'ul found himself on the other side of the conflict with rabbinic Judaism. The impact of Sha'ul's faith in Messiah was that he endured abuse and persecution from synagogue leaders of his time for the sake of teaching and proclaiming the Good News.

The influence of rabbinic Judaism spreads far and wide among the people Israel. That is a simple fact of Jewish life and *part* of who we are culturally. In fact, as we often point out in messianic synagogues, there are many extra-biblical Jewish symbols which strongly bear witness to Yeshua. Take the Hanukkiah, for example; or the Torah scrolls; or the *challah* bread. A messianic Rabbi never misses an opportunity to refer to Yeshua through the standard religious symbolism handed down to us by rabbinic Judaism. This should not be surprising to anyone, since Yeshua Himself came as a Jew.

However, there is an inherent discord and disharmony with rabbinic Judaism that cannot be reconciled by messianic Jews becoming more orthodox,

---

[34] Acts 9:1,2.
[35] Acts 9:3–19.

let alone by accepting the mythology of divine oral law. In fact, there are many things that are handed down by rabbinic Judaism which contradict the Scriptures, things which we as messianic Jews do not practice or believe, the chief of which is, obviously, the rabbinic claim that Yeshua is not the Messiah.

That claim is no small matter in rabbinic Judaism. As every messianic Jew of the modern era knows, the "mantra" of the rabbinic establishment regarding Messianic Judaism is that "Jewish people don't believe in Jesus." We've all heard it. And we all know it is a falsehood, as the very existence of the Messianic Jewish movement proves.

Today, there are hundreds of thousands of Jews worldwide who believe that Yeshua is Messiah, and the numbers are growing rapidly. Even critics of Messianic Judaism estimate there to be as many as 350,000 messianic Jews worldwide.[36] So much for the claim that Jewish people don't believe in Yeshua. Nevertheless, for the time being, it is the influence of the orthodox rabbinic establishment in the State of Israel which has adversely affected the right of Messianic Jews to make aliyah under the law of return.

---

[36] Posner, Sarah (November 29, 2012), "Kosher Jesus: Messianic Jews in the Holy Land", The Atlantic.

Orthodox Judaism – What is it?:

Belief in the rabbinic idea of a divine oral Torah is by no means the global standard in Judaism today. It is a belief found in Orthodox Judaism. Orthodox Judaism is represented by only a small minority of Jews today.

Orthodox Judaism is the continuation of the belief system created by the Pharisaic rabbinic Jews who drafted the Talmud. What is called "orthodox Judaism" today used to be just plain "Judaism." From the Talmudic era up until about the 1800's, there wasn't anything else that would be called "Judaism."

The term "orthodox" is often associated with observance. However, while orthodox Jews do tend to be the most observant Jews, that is not always the case, nor is it the defining factor in terms of what is meant by "orthodox." Orthodox refers not so much to practices, but to beliefs.

There are varied and quite diverse groups within what would normally be considered "orthodox Judaism." Unlike Reform and Conservative Judaism, Orthodox Judaism is not a denomination with a single governing body. What defines orthodox Judaism is a common belief in regard to the Torah. As progressive movements developed in Judaism in the 1800's, "Orthodox" is a term that was applied toward those

Jews who maintained a belief in the traditional approach to Torah. That is essentially how the term continues to be used today.

Hence, whatever variations, still what defines "orthodox Judaism" is the common belief in a Torah that is both written and oral; given by God to Moses at Sinai; and transmitted by a kind of divine revelation to the rabbis ever since. Without that belief, it isn't orthodox Judaism.

The reason orthodox Jews tend to be more observant than others, is because *halakha* in orthodox Judaism is seen as revealed from heaven. *Halakha* is therefore seen as binding and mandatory, not advisory nor subject to interpretation. *Halakha* is treated as an immutable revelation, not something to be interpreted, but, rather, understood.[37]

The most recent Pew study in 2013, called *A Portrait of Jewish Americans*, showed as follows: In the

---

[37] Comparatively, the position of Reform and Conservative Judaism on *halakha* is too complex and diverse to discuss here. While both might seem to give tacit approval to the orthodox claim that *halakha* is divine, neither approaches all *halakha* as binding. This tends to indicate non-belief in the orthodox notion that *halakha* is divine in nature. But definitive statements in this respect are typically avoided. We note that even the Tanakh, for many Reform and Conservative Jews, is not seen as divine, let alone the oral tradition. Reform Judaism sees *halakha* as advisory, not mandatory. See: Rabbi Mark Washofsky, "Reform Judaism and Halakha," https://www.myjewishlearning.com/article/reform-judaism-halakhah/.

United States, home to nearly half of the world's Jewish population, only about 10% of the Jewish population identifies as Orthodox. The largest groups, 41% identify with the Reform movement (including Reconstructionist and Renewal), while 18% identify with Conservative Judaism. About 31% identify as "nones," that is, no affiliation at all.[38]

In Israel, research shows that 9% of Jews in the land identify as ultra-orthodox, and 11% simply as religious. Meanwhile 44.3% identify as secular.[39]

While statistics can vary slightly from one survey to the next, it is nevertheless abundantly clear that orthodox rabbinic Judaism today has lost credibility with the Jewish people. It is just as spoken by the mouth of the prophet Jeremiah:

"For the shepherds are stupid! They have not sought Adonai. Therefore, they have not acted wisely, and all their flocks are scattered." [40]

Other than the slim minority of orthodox Jews in the U.S., and ultra-orthodox Jews in Israel, other Jews are extremely unlikely to believe the orthodox premise

---

[38]   http://www.pewforum.org/2013/10/01/jewish-american-beliefs-attitudes-culture-survey/

[39]   https://www.jewishvirtuallibrary.org/latest-population-statistics-for-israel

[40] Jer. 10:21.

that God gave an oral law to Moses which was then handed down by some divine impartation to the Rabbis. That premise, which has been a central tenet of Judaism for the centuries of the rabbinic era, has lost its foothold.

It is no coincidence that at the same time in history that the old Judaism is losing the ear of the people, God is restoring Jews to true biblical Judaism, by faith in Messiah Yeshua. The fact is, for God's salvation plan to fully unfold for the Jews, it is necessary to expose the oral Torah for what it is – a myth. A non-Torah.

What the Tanakh Says:

If an oral law was really given to Moses at Sinai, obviously Moses would've mentioned it in the written law. He didn't. Or at least it would've been mentioned somewhere later in the *Tanakh* (Old Testament Scriptures). It isn't.

The Tanakh says nothing whatsoever about an oral law given by God. But the Tanakh does repeatedly address the importance of the written Scriptures, and warns against adding to, or subtracting from them:

- *"You must not add to the word that I am commanding you or take away from it—in order to keep the mitzvot of ADONAI your God that I am commanding you"* (Deut. 4:2).
- *"Whatever I command you, you must take care to do—you are not to add to it or take away from it"* (Deut. 13:1).
- *"Every Word of God is purified. He is a shield to those who take refuge in Him. Do not add to His words, or else He will rebuke You and prove you a liar"* (Prov. 30:5,6).

The Tanakh also states that Moses wrote down the words God gave to him, without ever making any mention of an oral transmission that was not written down, let alone handed down generationally.

- *So Moses wrote down all the words of ADONAI, then rose up early in the morning, and built an altar below the mountain, along with twelve pillars for the twelve tribes of Israel"* (Ex. 24:4).
- *Then afterward he read all the words of the Torah—the blessing and the curse—according to all that is written in the book of the Torah. ³⁵ There was not a word of all that Moses commanded that Joshua did not read before all the assembly of Israel, including*

*the women and the little ones and the outsiders
walking among them"* (Josh. 8:34, 35).

- *This SEFER Torah (book of the Law) should not
depart from your mouth—you are to meditate on it
day and night, so that you may be careful to do
everything written in it. For then you will make your
ways prosperous and then you will be successful"*
(Joshua 1:8).

- *"Be very resolute to keep and to do all that is
written in the book of the Torah of Moses, so that
you may not turn aside from it to the right or to the
left..."* (Joshua 23:6).

The written Scriptures repeatedly refer to the
written Scriptures, but nowhere is there any mention of
an oral Torah. Why not? Because it didn't exist, but was
created later on in history by the rabbis.

It is clear from the Tanakh, that God instructed
His people to rely upon the written word in order to stay
firmly planted in faith and not be led astray. The myth
of a divinely-given oral law has led the people Israel
astray, taking our attention away from Scripture, by
paying heed instead to the sayings of the Rabbis.

What the New Testament Says:

It is clear from the New Testament that the oral Torah mythology was around in Yeshua's time. As previously mentioned, it is referred to as "the tradition of the elders."[41] Yeshua Himself was often confronted by religious leaders among the Pharisees who opposed Him on the ground that He did not follow the "tradition of the elders." Yeshua made it clear that the oral law was nothing more than the doctrine of men. For example, Yeshua said:

> *"On account of your tradition, you made void the Word of God. Hypocrites! Rightly did Isaiah prophesy about you, saying, 'This people honors Me with their lips, but their heart is far from Me. And in vain they worship Me, teaching as doctrines the commandments of men.'"*[42]

Hence, the Yeshua-movement and its progeny were not adherents of that tradition which is premised upon oral Torah. Yeshua further made it clear, just before He departed and entered into the heavens: *"All authority in heaven and on earth has been given to Me."*[43]

---

41 Mat. 15:2.
42 Mat. 15:6–9.
43 Mat. 28:18.

By saying "all authority" this meant that He alone is the Word of God made flesh. Therefore, a body of religious leaders who categorically deny that Yeshua is the Messiah are without authority, having cut themselves off from the Word of God, as a branch cut off from the tree.

That is not to say that Yeshua was against all Jewish tradition. He most certainly was not. It is to say that He was against the practice of treating the sayings of the Rabbis as if they were the Word of God. As Yeshua said, upbraiding those who cling to the oral law mythology:

"Having left behind the commandment of God, you hold on to the tradition of men."[44]

Yeshua was not only Jewish by birth, He also lived a Jewish life. He was Jewish in custom, culture and heritage. He did not abolish Jewish tradition. He often embraced and lived by it. Nevertheless, Yeshua opposed the elevation of tradition to divine status. So, do we as Jewish followers of Yeshua of the modern era.

Tradition has its place in every society. Messianic Jews do not find Jewish culture or tradition to be objectionable. We embrace it—but not if it conflicts with

---

[44] Mark 7:8.

Scripture. We also respect the efforts of our people to interpret and apply the Word of God to Jewish life. But man's word is not the Word of God.

The Pharisaic leaders who considered their word to be the Word of God were advocates of a kind of Torah that is nothing more than a non-Torah. In that respect, Yeshua opposed their teaching, as did the Apostles after Him, who relied upon the authority of Scripture. This was plain for them to see from Moses in the Torah, and throughout the Tanakh. It is also stated in the New Testament:

> *"All Scripture is inspired by God and useful for teaching, for reproof, for restoration, and for training in righteousness, so that the person belonging to God may be capable, fully equipped for every good deed." – 2 Tim. 3:16-17.*

<u>Chapter Two: The Bible</u>

Authority and Infallibility:

Messianic Jews believe that the Bible, consisting of the *Tanakh* (Holy Scriptures) and the later writings commonly known as the *B'rit Chadasha* (New Covenant), is the only authoritative and infallible Word of God. In Messianic Judaism, we recognize its divine inspiration, and accept its teachings as our final authority in all matters of faith and practice. The importance of the Bible cannot be overestimated. There is nothing to compare to it.

There is a parallel that can be made in the secular world which illustrates the importance of the Bible to people of faith. In the modern era, the "rule of law" is a standard to which the governments of civilized nations typically adhere. The "rule of law" is the idea that individuals, groups and even government itself shall submit to, obey and be governed by established law, as opposed to arbitrary action by an individual or a group of individuals. The "rule of law" requires a written law. Whether a constitution, or basic statutes enacted by legislative action, or both, the principle of government by "rule of law" is necessarily achieved by the enactment of a written law.

The Bible is the written Word of God. Comparatively, if the secular world follows such a precept as rule of law, based on a written code of law, how much more people of faith need to follow the written Scriptures.

[handwritten: Crescent shaped region in the middle east Israel, Syria, Egypt, Jordan, Parts of Turkey, Cypress, Iran]

*[handwritten: * Form of writing Manuscript]*

The Written Law:

During the time of the Patriarchs, as civilization began to emerge in the so-called "fertile crescent" of the middle east, the foundation stone of civilization was a written law code. Some of the earliest known legal codes written in cuneiform script were commonly found among the people of the fertile crescent, including the Sumerians, Babylonians, Assyrians, Elamites, Hurrians, Kassites and Hittites.[45]

The most famous of ancient cuneiform legal codes is the code of Hammurabi, which addressed common issues of law arising in both criminal and civil matters.

[handwritten: 6th king of Babylon]

[handwritten: 282 Rules - Commercial interactions set Fines + Punishments to meet justice Requirements]

[45] Encyclopedia Brittanica, Cuneiform Law. See: https://www.britannica.com/topic/cuneiform-law

Egypt also had a written law code, as did the Greeks, and the Romans, in the era of classical civilization.

Tribal societies which lacked written law were prone to rely upon the oral traditions of the tribal elders. Without any clear frame of reference, even the most impartial and well-intentioned judge or judicial body can easily err in arriving at a fair and just outcome. More commonly, the lack of a written law code leaves the door wide open to the problem of partial judges with selfish motives. The fact is, an oral body of law can be easily manipulated by people in power.

Hence, the importance of written law cannot be overestimated historically. The implementation of written law is a key building block of civilization, something which separated the civilized from the barbarians. Conversely, the ability of a society to collaborate together toward the higher aims of civilization is far more challenging when "justice" is left to the whim of an elite group of tribal elders following a presumed oral tradition.

The fundamental purpose of the written word, as exemplified in secular history, proves true in biblical history as well. The purpose and function of the written Bible has been particularly vital for the Jewish people, being a nation set apart and chosen by God to be blessing unto all nations. Every culture has its oral

Repent - To destroy the house —— Pictograph
give it up; change

55

traditions. Israel does too. However, in regard to the calling upon Israel, overreliance upon oral tradition would seriously impede the course of fulfillment. How much more when, in reference to the oral tradition of Jewish culture, a mythology of divine transmission is concocted by spiritual elders and is embraced by the people.

No Perfect Document:

That is not to say that the establishment of written law can guarantee justice. As we see in modern democratic Republics and/or Parliamentary Democracies, such as the U.S., Great Britain and the State of Israel, whether the written law is put forth as a constitution or body of basic laws, the written law itself is inevitably imperfect.

Even in the event of great written works such as the Magna Carta or the U.S. Constitution, for example, the documents are extremely well crafted, by men who earnestly sought the guidance and approval of God Almighty. Nevertheless, the result is imperfect. Because even for the most noble of human beings, in taking on the task of drafting written law, there will always be two key problems:

One, there is no perfect document written by the mind and the hand of human beings. The written law codes of even the greatest and most godly nations suffer from the fact that they are written by human beings. The drafters themselves might be men of God, but still men.

Secondly, even in the case of the most well-conceived written constitution, inevitably, the written law must be interpreted and rightly applied by human beings. And human beings are flawed.

Therefore, if the written law codes, which are the benchmark of the civilized world, cannot guarantee a just society, how much more a society that is ruled by oral tradition. It is well-established that confusion arises within a society which submits to be ruled by the whim of tribal elders, who act without regard to written law, on the ground that they know by oral tradition what is best for their particular society.

In the United States, for example, there is a real concern that a liberal judiciary might rise to power which interprets the Constitution not upon its plain meaning but based upon what they as an elite group of liberal intellectuals might feel is right for the country today. A good argument can be made that a decision like *Roe v. Wade*, which legalized abortion on the basis of the Fourth amendment, is exactly that type of phenomenon in which an elite group of people who "know better" impose their will over the whole of society by ignoring or redefining its written law.

The Law of Return – a Glaring Contradiction:

The modern State of Israel's approach to the Law of Return, as applied to messianic Jews, is another glaring example of how injustice can result when religious leaders and their oral tradition, at times, are permitted to supersede the clear meaning of the written law. The origin of the Law of Return is described on the website of the Israeli Knesset as follows:

> *"Zionist ideology was premised upon the reconstitution of the Jews as a free, self-determining nation in their own state. In recognition of this aspiration, Israel's Declaration of Independence declared that "The State of Israel will be open to the immigration of Jews and for the ingathering of exiles from all countries of their dispersion." In 1950, this principle was given shape as the Law of Return, enshrining this Zionist principle within Israeli law.*
>
> *The Law of Return did not stem from ideology alone; it was also a practical measure. In the wake of the*

Holocaust, the first act of the new Israeli government was to abolish all restrictions on Jewish immigration. Israel, the government declared, would provide Jews the world over with a haven from antisemitism.[46]

The Law of Return naturally gives rise to the question of "who is a Jew?" Under Israeli law, it is stated as follows:

"At present the definition is based on Hitler's Nuremberg Laws: the right of Return is granted to any individual with one Jewish grandparent, or who is married to someone with one Jewish grandparent."[47]

On its face, this law would seem straightforward enough, but as a result of the undue influence of orthodox rabbinic leaders upon Israeli public policy, the Israeli Supreme Court has allowed orthodoxy to define a law that is otherwise plain and clear. The impact is felt not only in regard to *aliyah* (Jewish immigration to Israel), but also orthodox rabbinic influence has given rise to contentious debate within Israeli society over issues of valid marriage. As is, no marriage performed in the State of Israel is considered valid unless conducted

---

[46] See, subheading: "Law of Return" at
http://knesset.gov.il/constitution/ConstMJewishState.htm
[47] Ibid.

by an orthodox Rabbi. Conversion to Judaism involves a similar issue. As the Knesset website further explains:

> *"To make matters more complicated, the Israeli Rabbinate, a purely Orthodox body, is far more stringent about its definition of who is a Jew, leaving thousands of 'Jewish' immigrants ineligible for marriage and unrecognized by the state authorities."*[48]

On Oct. 27th, 2018, the Tree of Life synagogue in Pittsburgh, was victimized by a mass shooting, killing 11 and injuring 7 during a Saturday Morning Shabbat service. Tree of Life is a member of the United Synagogue of Conservative Judaism (USCJ), which is the pre-eminent and largest conservative synagogue network in the world. Nevertheless, leaders of the orthodox community in Israel, as well as orthodox newspapers reporting on the incident, refused to refer to the Tree of Life synagogue as a "synagogue." Rather than acknowledge that the horrific anti-semitic mass murder had been carried out in a synagogue, Chief Ashkenazi Rabbi of Israel, David Lau, referred to the location as *"a place with a profound Jewish flavor."* [49]

---

[48] Ibid.

[49] Maltz, Judy, "Israel's Chief Rabbi Refuses to Call Pittsburgh Massacre Site a Synagogue Because It's non-Orthodox," Oct. 28th, 2018. https://www.haaretz.com/israel-news/.premium-israel-s-chief-rabbi-refuses-to-call-pittsburgh-massacre-site-a-

That incident serves to highlight the fundamental flaw with allowing religious elders to have undue influence on public policy and lawmaking. Within our own Jewish context, the question of being "Jewish," gets warped and convoluted when left to be defined by the ultra-orthodox, who have an agenda to bring all Jews under their purview and control.

Who is a Jew?

An amended version of the Law of Return was enacted in 1970, entitled the "Second Amendment to the Law of Return," which in essence affirmed the right of a Jew to make aliyah as before, but added the language: *"except for a person who has been a Jew and has voluntarily changed his religion."*

What exactly amounts to a "change of religion" is left undefined. But in common practice the orthodox rabbinate has interjected into public policy the halakhic view that a person who is Jewish by blood is legally considered "not Jewish" if he or she is a Jew who believes in Yeshua. Accordingly, the many Jewish people today who reject rabbinic Judaism as their religion, and/or have become Atheists or Buddhists, etc. are

---

synagogue-1.6601043 .

granted citizenship under the Law of Return, but a messianic Jew is denied.

Of course, during the Holocaust, the Nazis made no such distinction, and many thousands of Jewish believers in Yeshua perished along with the six million.[50] Hence, by allowing religious oral tradition to override the clear mandate of written law, an unjust and hypocritical result ensues. Thus, the law has been used to deny messianic Jews the right to make aliyah. This contradicts the stated purpose of the law, which is to provide a haven for Jews from anti-semitism in the wake of the Holocaust.

The influence of the oral law of the ultra-orthodox as applied within the context of the amendment to the Law of Return, creates an illogical conclusion as applied to Jewish believers in Yeshua; but, ironically, this effect contradicts rabbinic halakha itself. As David Clayman, a conservative Rabbi and director of the Israel office of the American Jewish Congress in Jerusalem, said in regard to the landmark court decisions lying behind this amendment:

---

[50] Dr. Mitch Glaser, President of Chosen People Ministries, states: *"The numbers of Jewish believers living in Europe prior to the Holocaust numbered in the hundreds of thousands, and most were either killed or moved to other parts of the globe."* See: Glaser, "Heroes of the Holocaust: Poland, the Warsaw Ghetto and Yeshua," March, 2012.

"By this ruling the law of the land contradicted Jewish law, since according to rabbinic halakhah, a Jew remains a Jew even if he is converted to another faith."[51]

Other Historical Examples:

In more extreme cases, every corrupt monarch, dictator or elite totalitarian group (as in Communist societies) in the modern era has risen to power on the basis of being able to dictate what the law is or is not in their particular society. Whomever controls the law, controls the society.

Therefore, in the whole of human history, the modus operandi of every tyrant, dictator or power group with an agenda to exploit the people for personal gain necessarily involves one key element. Specifically, they presume upon themselves the authority – whether by mythological propaganda, or by force of arms, or by both – to supersede the mandate of the written law.

A Nation Unlike Any Other:

Biblically speaking, Israel is a nation unlike any other. True, like every ancient culture, the Jewish people

---

[51] Clayman, "The Law of Return Reconsidered," Jerusalem Letters of Lasting Interest, No. 318 18 Tammuz 5755/16 July 1995, www.jcpa.org/jl/hit01.htm.

developed a legal system for judging conflicts and dealing with matters of controversy. However, Israel's written law, is radically unique from all other nations. For the written law given to Israel was given directly by God.

Israel as created by God is the only nation on earth whose "constitution" is indeed a perfect document. For unlike other nations, Israel did not create its own written law. It is not the product of a democratic society. It did not come through parliamentary assembly nor through scholarship. It did not come by legislative act, nor by the decree of a wise old elder. Israel received its written word directly from the Lord.

For beginning with the five books of Moses, the entirety of the written Word of God – the Bible – was given to Israel. It was given by God to one nation, meant as a blessing to all nations.

There simply is nothing to compare to it. The Bible is inerrant truth, as the Word of God given to mankind in written form, to lead many to salvation and to provide a means for discipleship, spiritual growth and development of those who receive its message and way of life. The purpose of the written word is clear, as Sha'ul said to Timothy:

"From childhood you have known the sacred writings that are able to make you wise, leading to salvation through trusting in Messiah Yeshua. All Scripture is inspired by God and useful for teaching, for reproof, for restoration, and for training in righteousness, so that the person belonging to God may be capable, fully equipped for every good deed." [52]

The New Covenant makes clear the point that the Word of God, which is the Son of God, that is from the beginning, "became flesh and dwelt among us."[53] From Genesis to Revelation, the Bible bears witness to Messiah Yeshua, who is the Lord God from the beginning. It is the gift of God to help humanity come to know the Lord our Savior who, at the appointed time, became one of us.

The messianic Jewish movement – whether in the First Century CE or in this modern era – is the result of the outpouring of the Spirit of God:

"And it shall be in the last days,' says God, 'that I will pour out My Ruach on all flesh. Your sons and your daughters shall prophesy, your young men shall see visions, and your old men shall dream dreams." [54]

---

[52] 2 Tim. 3:15–17.
[53] See: John 1:1–3 and John 1:14.
[54] Acts 2:17, Joel 3:1.

℘   Nevertheless, as the Spirit is poured out upon all flesh, our means for coming to salvation, and the foundation for growth in the knowledge of the One who came from heaven in human form[55] – Messiah Yeshua – is the written word given to mankind via the Holy Scriptures of the Bible.

God did not give an oral, non-written body of instruction nor would such a thing be necessary to enable people to understand the Scripture. For the meaning of Scripture and the essential message of salvation is not hidden, but plain on its face. Some don't see it, but it is God Himself, by means of the outpouring of His Spirit, which enables us to see it. Just as Yeshua did when He was still with His talmidim, He continues to do by sending forth the Ruakh HaKodesh:

"Then He opened their minds to understand the Scriptures."[56]

There is no secret body of knowledge out there which was orally transmitted by God. This is why there is no reference to such a thing in the Scriptures.

---

[55] Phil. 2:7: *"But He emptied Himself—taking on the form of a servant, becoming the likeness of men and being found in appearance as a man."*
[56] Luke 24:45.

A Family Becomes a Nation:

God separated a family unto himself by calling forth Abraham, Isaac, and Jacob.[57] God gave Abraham a great name. But without a written law, the tribal family of Abraham could never become a nation. It is through the medium of a written law by which a tribal family becomes a nation.

Therefore, in delivering Israel up out of Egypt, the Lord gave Israel its national identity by giving His word in written format. The Bible is the gift of God to Israel, given for the benefit of all mankind. For eventually, all nations would have access to the Word of God, as given in writing to the nation chosen by God to receive it.

The ten commandments were written upon stone tablets by the finger of God himself.[58] The rest of the Torah was written down by Moses as the words were spoken to him by God. This procedure is well-documented in the written words of the Torah.

It began with the giving of what the Torah itself calls the *"aseret ha-d'varim,"*[59] better known as the ten commandments. After the ten commandments were spoken by God from the cloud at Sinai, in the hearing of all Israel, as described in Exodus 20, Moses then went

---

[57] Gen. 12:2-3: *"I will make you into a great nation...and all peoples on earth will be blessed through you."*

[58] Ex. 34:1,2.

[59] See: Ex. 34:28, Deut. 4:13 and Deut. 10:4.

up into the cloud. There he received the *mishpatim* (ordinances), which were the first body of law from God, with instructions to write them down in a scroll and put them before the people Israel:

> *"Now these are the ordinances which you will set before them."*[60]

After receiving the various *mishpatim*, as documented by the ensuing three chapters in Ex. 21-23, the Torah states that Moses came down the mountain. It then describes how Moses presented the Word of God to the people, emphasizing the fact that Moses wrote down ALL the words God spoke to him:

> *"So Moses wrote down **all the words of Adonai.**"*[61]

And then, a few verses later:

> *"He took **the scroll of the Covenant** and read it in the hearing of the people."*[62]

After that, God called Moses up the mountain again, in order to receive the "*luchot habrit,*" the tablets of the covenant. Even though God had already spoken

---

[60] Ex. 21:1.

[61] Ex. 24:4 (emphasis added).

[62] Ex. 24:7.

the ten commandments in the hearing of the whole people Israel, now God gave Moses those words written upon tablets of stone, not by Moses' hand but by the finger of God Himself. Thus, the Lord says:

> "Then Adonai said to Moses, "Come up to Me on the mountain and stay there, and I will give you the tablets of stone with the Torah and the mitzvot, which I have written so that you may instruct them."[63]

Therefore, throughout the Torah, it continually makes the point that God gave His word to Moses to be conveyed in written format. God gave the written word to Israel in order to fulfill his purpose as stated to Abraham, to make from one man a great nation, for the benefit of all mankind.[64]

Thus, the writing down of the Word of God began with Moses for the express purpose of God's plan to create a nation from the family of Abraham. For as history has proven, oral tradition is tribal, but nations are constituted by the written word. Tribal families come and go, along with their ever-changing oral traditions that leave no record. But nations, like words committed to parchment paper, tend to endure. And

---

[63] Ex. 24:12.
[64] Ibid. See also Ex. 19:6 – "You will be to Me a kingdom of kohanim and a holy nation."

even after they fade, their impression upon history is clearly made.

Put It In Writing:

Israel's nationhood was established by God giving His word to the appointed prophets of His chosen nation, with instructions to put it in writing. This was accomplished at first with Moses. The procedure by which it happened is documented in the Torah. God gave His word to Moses with the imperative to write it down and then give it to Israel:[65]

*"Moses **wrote down this Torah** and gave it to the kohanim, the sons of Levi who carry the Ark of the Covenant of Adonai, and to all the elders of Israel."*[66]

After Moses completed his ministry, the word of the Lord came to Joshua to give him counsel in terms of how to carry on after Moses. Basically, God told Joshua to study the book that Moses wrote. Obviously, if there was an oral law given to Moses, Joshua would need to study that too, wouldn't he? There is no mention of it.

---

[65] Ex. 34:27: *"Then the LORD said to Moses, 'Write down these words, for in accordance with these words I have made a covenant with you and with Israel.'"* See also: Ex. 24:4, Ex. 24:12, Num. 33:2, Deut. 1:5, Deut. 4:4.

[66] Deut. 31:9 (emphasis added).

Because it doesn't exist. This is recorded in the opening verses of the book of Joshua. God said to Joshua:

> "*Only be very strong, and resolute to observe diligently* **the Torah which Moses, My servant, commanded you.** *Do not turn from it to the right or to the left, so you may be successful wherever you go.* **This book of the Torah** *should not depart from your mouth—you are to meditate on it day and night, so that you may be careful to do everything written in it. For then you will make your ways prosperous and then you will be successful."*[67]

It is the "sefer Torah" (book or scroll of the Torah) that God tells Joshua to meditate in day and night because there is no other Torah. Any other is a non-Torah. It does not exist. The tradition which says that Moses also gave an oral Torah to Joshua, who then passed it onward,[68] is a self-attesting claim which is without any reliable source. It is nowhere found in the pages of the Bible, and in every respect the Bible testifies against it.

This process that began with Moses continued thereafter until the entirety of the Bible was given to Israel as God spoke His word unto the prophets which

---

[67] Joshua 1:7- (emphasis added).
[68] See, Avot 1:1.

He appointed. Some of them were also Judges, Kings, Psalmists, and Apostles of Messiah.

It is the written Word of God, which was given by the Lord unto Israel which makes Israel unique in accordance with the calling of God to be a nation which is a light to all other nations.[69] For while every nation on earth might have its own unique written law code, there is none like Israel, whose written document is the actual Word of God Himself.

Therefore, in the fulfillment of God's plan, when Israel lives according to the Word of God, then, too, the nations of the world will come to the knowledge of the Lord. For the nations will be drawn to discover and learn from Israel's God-given manifesto, the Bible, which was written down by the prophets of Israel for the good of all mankind.

The importance of the written Scriptures cannot be overstated. Today, the Bible has gone forth to the whole world and can be studied in every language on the face of the earth.

The Lord gave Israel the word in written format. God's prophetic plan to provoke the nations to come unto the knowledge of God through His written word is first set forth in the Torah:

---

[69] Is. 49:6.

"See, I have taught you decrees and laws as the Lord my God commanded me, so that you may follow them in the land you are entering to take possession of it. Observe them carefully, for this will show your wisdom and understanding to the nations, who will hear about all these decrees and say, "Surely this great nation is a wise and understanding people." What other nation is so great as to have their gods near them the way the Lord our God is near us whenever we pray to him? And what other nation is so great as to have such righteous decrees and laws as this body of laws I am setting before you today?"[70]

There is not now, nor has there ever been a plan of God to teach an "oral law" to Israel nor to the world. What God gave to the world, via the Jewish people, was the Word of God written down into the format of the Bible. Accordingly, both Old and New Testaments were eventually imparted to the whole world in every language. The function of the written Scriptures, as translated into every language, is vitally important in the scenario of the end times, immediately before Messiah's return.

Those who claim to be teachers of a divinely-given oral law typically like to posit themselves as

---

[70] Deut. 4:5-8.

holding some secret knowledge that is otherwise hidden from the world, not found in Scripture, and revealed only to an elite cast of orthodox scholars who supposedly transmitted it from Moses, through the centuries of rabbinic Judaism, right down to today. They would have their adherents believe that the written Scriptures cannot be understood without the oral law. Therefore, in effect, they give oral law superior authority over the Bible. Then, the student who buys into the idea that it is necessary to study oral law for purposes of understanding the Scriptures, will have to submit himself or herself to the "masters" that purport to have obtained this body of knowledge from God by divine transmission.

The mythology of a divine oral law as sort of the "Rosetta Stone" to understanding Scripture is not only completely without merit, but also can become a dangerous premise in which the submitted person can easily become the subject of manipulation by persons with selfish motives. After all, we are talking about men who claim to have authority equal to the Word of God.

The approach to this can vary. In any case, those who put forth the claim are at best disingenuous; and in the worst case, flat-out deceptive and self-aggrandizing. In any case, no such oral body of knowledge exists, nor would it be necessary to have been given an oral law in order to understand the written Word of God. Those who claim there is such a necessity are basing their claim on a false premise.

Shoftim:

Every society that lives by a written law is also tasked with the responsibility to rightly interpret and apply it to their communal life. Inevitably, this task becomes the role of *shoftim* (judges). The rise or fall of a secular society established even upon the most noble of efforts to draft a written law, ultimately depends upon an honest and righteous judiciary to interpret and apply it.

In this respect, biblical Israel was no exception. Therefore, included in the written word given by God to Moses at Sinai, is a section having to do with the establishment of judges and the setting up of something that functioned as a judicial system. It states:

> *"Judges and officers you are to appoint within all your gates that Adonai your God is giving you, according to your tribes; and they are to judge the people with righteous judgment."*[71]

---

[71] Deut. 16:18.

The need for *shoftim* (judges) of a wise and righteous nature is fundamentally necessary in order to mete out justice. Receiving the law from God was not enough. The law of God needed to be implemented into Jewish life. Hence, righteous judges were vital to Israel's ability to fulfill its calling as "am segulah," God's own peculiar "treasured people." As it says:

> *"Justice, justice you must pursue, so that you may live and possess the land that Adonai your God is giving you."*[72]

In that verse, the Torah itself makes clear that the failure on the part of the *shoftim* is directly connected to dwelling in *eretz Yisrael* (the land of Israel). Exile has occurred twice in our national history. There are perhaps multiple reasons which can be fairly discussed. But the failure of the judiciary, culminating in the rejection of the Messiah two thousand years ago, is without doubt a key reason, if not the main one.

It is plain to see from a cursory glance at the historical chain, that the second Jewish diaspora was intimately connected to the rejection of Messiah by an elite group of corrupt and spiritually bankrupt religious leaders, who abused their position in the *Sanhedrin*

---

[72] Deut. 16:20.

(Jewish high court) to wrongfully accuse and convict Yeshua of blasphemy, as well as to conspire with the Romans to carry out a sentence of death by crucifixion.

The second diaspora, therefore, was precipitated by the rejection and crucifixion of Messiah Yeshua during about the 30's CE. The same generation witnessed the Roman Wars and consequent destruction of the Temple by the Romans in 70 CE, just as prophesied by Yeshua.[73]

The fall of the Temple initiated the second diaspora. This tragedy raised the hope of Jewish people everywhere for Israel's salvation via the Messiah. That climate gave rise to the designation by Rabbi Akiva of a false messiah – Bar Kokhba – and the revolt against the Romans that happened during 132–136 CE based upon the hope that Bar Kokhba indeed was the salvation of the people Israel.

The recognition and proclamation by the Jewish religious establishment of Bar Kokhba as the Messiah was a grave mistake that led to one of the worst tragedies in Jewish history. Nothing can ever excuse the atrocities carried out by the Romans against the Jews following the Bar Kokhba revolt. However, it should also be understood that the "judicial" error of recognizing false messiahs has plagued our Jewish people from the

---

[73] Mark 13:1,2; Mat. 24:1,2.

time that Yeshua was rejected, throughout the ensuing centuries of Jewish history.[74]

Furthermore, the same error continues to be facilitated today by the rabbinic leadership, which presumes authority through the oral law, without reference to the written Scriptures, to claim who is and who is not the Messiah. Accordingly, the true Messiah and Savior, Yeshua, remains unrecognized by the rabbinic community, while other individuals are believed by the orthodox to be the Messiah, who in no way fit the bill that is described in the Scriptures.

In the case of Bar Kokhba, all Jews – both in the land and in the diaspora, whether followers of Bar Kokhba or not – were deeply impacted by the official, national recognition of Bar Kokhba as Messiah. Despite the valiant fight put up by the Jews against the mighty Romans, it was put down by the Romans in 135 CE. Many were put to death. All were banned from Jerusalem. Most Jews who survived were exiled.

Thus, Israel's second diaspora clearly was connected to and precipitated by the failure of the *shoftim* which had authority through the Jewish court system to recognize Yeshua as Messiah. Opting instead to designate a false messiah, and to go on creating a religion which was not the "Judaism" of the written

[74] See: Mat. 24:4-14. Yeshua warns of false Messiahs who will come after Him.

Word of God, this brought calamity upon the whole Jewish nation.

Talmud, and later rabbinical writings, put forth many reasons attempting to explain why the second Temple was destroyed, which led eventually to a second diaspora. The key reason given by them is "*sinat chinam*" or "baseless hatred." But this is only a half-truth.

True, the First and Second Century CE was a time period in Jewish history marked by rampant infighting among the various political factions and religious sects of the Jewish people. However, it was the hatred levied against one group in particular – the messianic Jews – which was the main cause of strife. Messianic Jews were persecuted by Rome, but unlike most Jews, they could find little safety among their own people. In fact, beginning in the First Century, Messianic Jews were persecuted by the Jewish religious establishment. They were put out of the synagogues, hunted down, imprisoned, and even put to death.

In the second century, it can be reasonably presumed that messianic Jews, as believers in Yeshua, did not follow after Bar Kokhba. This probably caused them to be even further alienated from the prevailing Jewish pharisaic leadership. No group among the Jews was hated like the messianics.

Gamaliel, a Pharisee, and one of the great Talmudic scholars, as recorded in the Book of Acts, may have had a momentary insight to the great danger of persecuting the messianic Jews:

> "So now I tell you, stay away from these men and leave them alone. For if this plan or undertaking is of men, it will come to an end; but if it is of God, you will not be able to stop them. **You might even be found fighting against God.**"[75]

Gamaliel was correct, but unfortunately, Gamaliel's admonition was not followed through. The *sinat chinam*, or baseless hatred by the religious establishment against messianic Jews continued and increased. That resulted in rejection and persecution of the messianic Jews by their own Jewish brothers. Nevertheless, the Jewish body of believers in Yeshua continued to grow. So, too, the divide grew between messianic Jews and rabbinic Judaism.

Many of the explanations for the fall of the second Temple and for the second diaspora that are given in the Talmud and other rabbinical writings have come to be accepted as fact by the Jewish people at large. Obviously, the rejection of Yeshua as Messiah is not one of the

---

[75] Acts 5:38,39 (emphasis added).

reasons given. Instead, the message transmitted by orthodox rabbinism does not own up to the core issue of what went wrong. Instead it maintains the façade that it has the solution. If everyone will sit at the feet of the masters and learn Torah (oral and written), then God will be pleased, we will have *tikkun olam*, the Messiah will come to bring Jews back from diaspora, and there will at last be peace on earth. This is the same tune that has been sung by orthodox Judaism for nearly two thousand years.

Yet here we are in the modern era, Jews have been returning to eretz Yisrael, the Jewish State is established and being rebuilt, and the State of Israel is not a creature of orthodox Judaism. Contemporaneously, a growing number of Jews worldwide are declaring that Yeshua is the Messiah. This leaves the orthodox Jewish rabbinic leadership somewhat miffed. And as they jockey for position, they are losing the ear of the jewish people, who after nearly two thousand years, have become disillusioned with the religious system, and are no longer listening.

In fact, the rabbinical writings are not reliable in determining why the Temple was destroyed, nor why the diaspora occurred. The attempts of those writings to explain what brought about the end of the second Temple and the exile that followed is a self-perpetuating legend. It is continually offering affirmation toward its own mythological premise of a divine oral law allegedly given by God to the Jewish religious establishment. It is an oral law that is written by the very hand of the ones who claim that God gave it to them. It offers rationalizations which are meant to give credence to the very system that failed the Jewish people to begin with. They claim Messiah will come. Then they point to messiahs who are not the Messiah. In like manner, they point to an oral Torah that is a non-Torah.

The truth is that the real Messiah has come, just as Moses in the Torah said He would:

> "ADONAI *your God will raise up for you a prophet like me from your midst—from your brothers. To him you must listen...I will raise up a prophet like you for them from among their brothers. I will put My words in his mouth, and he will speak to them all that I command him. Now whoever does not listen to My words that this prophet speaks in My Name, I Myself will call him to account."* [76]

The Messiah came as a Jew, and He came to the Jews. A great many of His own people believed in Him.

---

[76] Deut. 18:15 and Deut. 18:18-19. See also: Romans 11:25-26, and 29.

Thousands of Jews became followers of Yeshua. They brought the message first throughout the land of Israel, then to the Jewish communities of the diaspora, and then also to the Gentiles. The first messianic Jews faced not only Roman persecution, but eventually, Christian anti-Semitism sought to erase all Jews and all semblance of Jewishness from the faith which messianic Jews brought from Israel and spread among the Gentiles throughout the Roman Empire.[77]

Hence, Israel was exiled and scattered abroad following the Temple's destruction by the Romans, and again following the Bar Kokhba revolt. But just as stated by Moses in the Torah, following a period of exile, the promise of Israel's prophetic, end-time restoration remains irrevocable:

"Then ADONAI *your God will bring you back from captivity and have compassion on you, and He will return and gather you from all the peoples where* ADONAI *your God has scattered you. Even if your*

---

[77] Since the topic of this work is not Christian anti-semitism, the important theme of errors by the Church historically will not be treated in detail here. Suffice it to say here, however, that the ability of Jews to see Yeshua as Messiah has been greatly hampered by Christian replacement Theology, together with the horrific history of Christian anti-Semitism that came about as a result of it. We note, sadly, that Christian anti-semitism still lingers somewhat to this very day, as illustrated by major Christian denominations engaging in support of BDS measures against Israel.

outcasts are at the ends of the heavens, from there ADONAI your God will gather you, and from there He will bring you. ADONAI your God will bring you into the land that your fathers possessed, and you will possess it; and He will do you good and multiply you more than your fathers."[78]

The promise of Israel's prophetic end-time restoration is based not in an oral law but in the Scriptures which bear witness to the Messiah. This is why Israel's end-time restoration to the land has begun to happen contemporaneously with the messianic Jewish revival. Jewish return to the land and return to Messiah are intertwined like strands of DNA.

It should be understood, therefore, that the real Messiah and His Jewish progeny were rejected two thousand years ago by the religious leaders who, acting as judges, cast aside the authority of the written word because they felt threatened by it. This all happened just as prophesied by David in the Tanakh:

"The stone the builders rejected has become the cornerstone. It is from ADONAI: it is marvelous in our eyes!"[79]

---

[78] Ex. 30:3-5.
[79] Psalm 118:22,23.

What followed thereafter was the creation of a new Judaism, not found in the Scriptures. Instead, theirs is a Judaism based on a mythological premise that put the creators of it – the Rabbis – at the helm of leadership.

In a time of great instability and fear, the Pharisaic rabbinic leaders seized upon a political vacuum and assumed upon themselves the role of *shoftim*. What they set up has attempted to thwart the effort of messianic Jews to declare the gospel message to Israel. Many Jews have come to know Yeshua in spite of the opposition of the rabbis. But the Bible bears witness as do the facts of history that standing at the very core of what brought calamity, destruction and exile upon the people Israel was spiritually-blinded *shoftim*. They were partial in judgment and blinded by their desire for power and influence both with the Romans and over the Jewish people as well. They added and subtracted from the written Word of God. It happened exactly as Torah said it would happen when *shoftim* are motivated by the wrong intentions:

> *"You are not to twist justice—you must not show partiality or take a bribe, for a bribe blinds the eyes of the wise and distorts the words of the righteous. Justice, justice you must pursue, **so that you may live***

and possess the land that Adonai your God is giving you."[80]

The day is at hand in which the eyes of Israel are being opened. The mythological premise of a divine oral Torah is being exposed for what it is – a non-Torah. As God pours out His Spirit upon the Jewish people in the end times, the truth of God's word is being found where it is – in the written Word of God, as recorded in the pages of the Bible.

Three Branches, One Tree:

The nation of Israel was created by the Word of God. The word was reduced to writing by the command of God, by the hand of Moses. To reiterate, the Torah states plainly and throughout, that Moses received the Word of God and wrote it down. He then gave the *sefer Torah* (Torah scroll) to Israel in writing. Moses also publicly read the *sefer Torah* and taught it to Israel.[81] The tradition of public reading of the Torah and *haftarah* or prophetic readings from the Tanakh, has carried on

---

[80] Deut. 16:19,20 (*emphasis added*).

[81] Ex. 34:27: "*Then ADONAI said to Moses, "Write these words, for based on these words I have cut a covenant with you and with Israel."* See also: Deut. 4:44 – "V'zot haTorah asher sam Moshe, lifnei b'nei Yisrael." (*This is the Torah, which Moses set before Bnei-Yisrael*).

through the generations.[82] Today the reading of the Torah and haftarah continues in modern day synagogues, including messianic synagogues.

The life and the governing authority of Israel is the Lord Himself. Like three branches of a tree, connected to one vine, the common concept of three branches of one government is found in the written Scriptures. Isaiah, for example, referenced the Judicial, Legislative and Executive branches in stating:

"For Adonai is our Judge, Adonai is our Lawgiver, Adonai is our King— He will save us!"[83]

More specifically, the three branches of one government are clearly and succinctly laid out in the Torah. First, repeatedly and throughout the Torah is set forth the legislative work of giving the law. God gave the law to Moses, with instructions to write it down and set it before Israel.

Second, it sets forth the law of the judicial branch. God told Moses to set up a judiciary consisting of righteous, impartial judges.[84]

---

[82] In Nehemiah 8, for example, the sefer Torah was read in the hearing of the people who returned from the captivity in Babylon. This was instrumental in reviving the Jewish people at that time. No mention is made of any oral teaching being taught to the people.

[83] Is. 33:22.

[84] Deut. 16:19,20 and Deut. 17:8–13.

Third, in the verses immediately following, the Lord sets forth the law of the Executive branch:

"When you come to the land that Adonai your God is giving you, possess it and dwell in it, and you say, 'I will set a king over me, like all the nations around me,' you will indeed set over yourselves a king, whom Adonai your God chooses."[85]

In the government of the nation of God, the key to it is that the whole house exists upon the authority of the written Word of God. The judges are charged with the duty to interpret and rightly apply the word that Moses wrote down. And the King's success or failure as the chief executive leader will depend upon his learning the written Word of God:

"Now when he sits on the throne of his kingdom, he is to write for himself a copy of this Torah on a scroll, from what is before the Levitical kohanim. It will remain with him, and he will read in it all the days of his life, in order to learn to fear Adonai his God and keep all the words of this Torah and these statutes. Then his heart will not be exalted above his brothers, and he will not turn from the commandment to the

---

[85] Deut. 17:14,15.

right or to the left—so that he may prolong his days in his kingship, he and his sons, in the midst of Israel.[86]

It is important to note that the King is to learn the written Torah. No mention is made of the King's need to be learning "oral Torah," (since there is no such thing). But, rather, what makes a King a good leader, as opposed to one who leads the people into a time of backsliding, is that the King is to take the Word of God as written down by Moses, and write a copy of the *sefer Torah* for himself and learn it. His good leadership will depend on it. And in this manner, through the Word of God written down, the Lord reigns in every branch of government, and the land is governed by the power of God's word.

On Par With The Word of God:

There is clearly much wisdom and insight to be found in the Jewish rabbinic writings. Nothing said herein is intended in any way to suggest or advocate a wholesale dismissal of that body of work. That would be foolishness of a high order. What ought to be dismissed is the notion that it was given by God in the same sense as the written Tanakh.

---

[86] Deut. 17:18–20.

The pages of Jewish history are marked with many great individuals who served as spiritual leaders. Many of the rabbis have been wise, righteous, discerning, loving, kind, decent human beings who love God. Nevertheless, there is no excuse for the error of rabbinic Judaism in putting the word of men on par with the Word of God. Simply put, no matter how wise or intelligent or great that a man might be, when the word of a man is seen as being equal to the Word of God, this is a grave mistake.

Yet, rabbinic Judaism has created a belief system which puts the word of man on the level of the Word of God. Due to the centrality of that belief and practice within rabbinic Judaism which puts man's word on the level of the divine, much of rabbinic Jewish scholarship is aimed at meeting that very objective of proving itself to be the Word of God. Moreover, in actual practice, what has occurred in orthodoxy is that the word of the rabbis is considered to be not only equal to, but greater than the written Word of God.

This process of elevating the word of the rabbis as if the Word of God was given great thrust, historically, through the drafting of the Talmud. The Talmud is the main body of Jewish oral tradition reduced to written form. As stated previously, it evolved at first via the Mishna (finished about 200 CE), then later with the addition of Gemara (finished about 500 CE). The writers of the Talmud went to great lengths to craft a voluminous written work, spanning centuries of Jewish history, which documents and records the sayings of the rabbis. The Talmud records rabbinic decisions, opinions, and stories which oftentimes provide interesting insight regarding the interpretation and application of Scripture. But at other times, the narrative involves rabbis engaging in complete speculation and conjecture, far beyond anything connected to the Scriptures.

It should be understood that the objective of the Talmud was not merely to document the wise sayings of the rabbis. Instead, the Talmudic recording process was very much devoted to establishing the authority of those who were creating it, i.e. the rabbinic establishment. In this respect, the Talmud is self-laudatory and self-attesting in nature. It has, for example, no source other than itself for making its central claim of being divine in nature.

By writing down the sayings of the Rabbis, the Talmud seeks not just to make a record of ancient rabbinic wisdom, but to establish the sayings of those Rabbis as if they were literally the Word of God. This idea of the word of the Rabbis being the actual Word of God is the mythical fiber upon which the non-Torah of rabbinic Judaism was created. Conceptually, it is first stated in the Mishna, Avot 1:1:

"Moses received the Torah from Sinai and gave it over to Joshua; Joshua to the Elders; the Elders to the Prophets; and the Prophets gave it over to the Men of the Great Assembly."

Typically, in rabbinic thinking, the "Torah" mentioned in the above quote from the Mishna is meant as a reference to the supposed "oral Torah" that Moses received at Sinai. A litany of self-laudatory explanations found nowhere in the Bible are found both in the Talmud itself and in later rabbinic writings which purport to explain how the "oral law" was transmitted from Moses through particular sages of each generation, right up to the present day.

Within rabbinic Judaism, there are different approaches and various beliefs about the oral law. However, it is commonplace to overemphasize the sayings of the rabbis. The written Word of God is marginalized and given a smaller place, in favor of the word of the Rabbis.

The prevailing religious leadership in orthodox Judaism has created a body of Jewish thought which at times does resonate and reflect the wisdom of the Lord.

It does in some ways reflect the glory of God, as well as the rich biblical heritage of the Jewish people. This cannot and should not be denied.

What must be denied is the mythology of a divine oral law which effectively turns men into gods. This is a grave error, and it has caused Jewish people generally to be misled. The opinions of men are not equivalent to, let alone greater than the Word of God. What the rabbis have done, historically, is they have created a non-Torah and passed it off as Torah, using the non-Torah to try and prove its own existence.

Mishneh Torah:

Written nearly one thousand years after the Mishna, another key rabbinic work is the *Mishneh Torah* by Maimonides. He is also known as Rabbi Moshe ben Maimon, and by the acronym "RaMBaM," and is probably the most influential writer in rabbinic Judaism since the Talmud. His magnum opus, *Mishneh Torah*, which literally means "restatement of the Law," was written during about ten years from 1170–1180 CE. Many see it as even more important than the Talmud in that everything said in the Talmud can be found in a more concise form in the *Mishneh Torah*.

In any case, *Mishneh Torah* is essentially an effort to codify and simplify the vast body of Talmudic literature in a format that would be relatively easier and more coherent for Jewish people living in the diaspora to learn. Not that *Mishneh Torah* is short or simple, but relatively speaking, a restatement of the law is meant to be a simpler version of the great body it is restating. And this task Maimonides accomplished with brilliance and excellence. In just ten years he restated over one thousand years of rabbinic Jewish thought. Comparatively, the drafting of the Talmud took over three hundred years to complete.

Maimonides himself seemed to claim that his work in restating the oral law superseded the Talmud:

> *"I have called this work the restatement of the oral law (Mishneh Torah), for a person reads the written law first, and then reads this work, and knows from it the entire Oral Law, without needing to read any other book between them."*[87]

The greatness of the work that Maimonides accomplished for the Jewish people who had been in diaspora for over one thousand years, should not be underestimated nor underappreciated. Nevertheless,

---

[87] Maimonides, *Mishneh Torah*, Intro., verse 42.

error is error and it has to be pointed out. In drafting *Mishneh Torah*, Maimonides did not balk at the opportunity to restate the essential premise of rabbinic Judaism, that this body of knowledge is actually the Word of God.

From the very outset, in his introduction to *Mishneh Torah*, Maimonides opens with this self-attesting statement, which purports to be based on Ex. 24:12. He states:

> *1- All the commandments that were given to Moshe at Sinai were given together with their interpretation, as it is written "and I will give thee the Tables of Stone, and the Law, and the Commandment" (Exodus 24:12). "Law" is the Written Law; and "Commandment" is its interpretation: We were commanded to fulfill the Law, according to the Commandment. And this Commandment is what is called the Oral Law.*[88]

To suggest that the word "mitzvah" (commandment) in the Torah is a reference to "oral law" is indeed far-fetched. Rambam's suggested interpretation of Exodus 24:12 presented in the opening salvo of *Mishneh Torah* is the typically speculative and imaginative stuff put forth in the Talmud to try and

---

[88] Maimonides, *Mishneh Torah*, Introduction, verse 1.

establish the murky idea that God gave an oral Torah to Moses. The word "mitzvah" occurs throughout the Torah and the Tanakh, but nowhere is it used in a way to refer to an oral law. It does refer repeatedly to the commandments God gave to Moses which Moses wrote down in a scroll.

A myth cannot prove its own veracity by claiming it is not a myth. The non-Torah cannot by its man-made claims of divinity prove itself to be the Torah of God. This is why the "proofs" for the authenticity of oral law always come only from oral law itself, as in the case of the opening line in *Mishneh Torah*.

Thus, the Rambam in his Intro to *Mishneh Torah* informs the student of Torah up front in terms of why one ought to engage in the study of what is written in this book. It's like saying: "Everything that you are about to read here in this book is not my word, but it is the Word of God."

Rambam then goes on to explain the whole litany, as found in the *Mishna* (Avot 1:1) of how Moses supposedly received an oral Torah from God, and then conveyed it to Joshua and so forth. The restatement by Rambam of this legendary Talmudic account, which was already fixated in orthodox rabbinic thinking thanks to the Talmud, now gained further credence via Rambam's *Mishneh Torah*. That is how we got to where we are today in orthodox rabbinism. As Rambam continued in the next two verses of his intro:

> "*2 – The whole of the Law was written down by Moshe Our Teacher before he died, in his own hand...*
>
> *3 – But the Commandment, which is the interpretation of the Law--he did not write it down, but gave orders concerning it to the elders, to Yehoshua, and to all the rest of Israel, as it is written "all this word which I command you, you must take care to do ..."* (Deuteronomy 13:1). For this reason, it is called Torah sheba'al peh (Oral Law).*"

It is indeed curious that in quoting from Deut. 13:1, *Mishneh Torah* omits the second part of that verse, printed in bold below. The full verse states:

> "*All this word which I command you, you must take care to do—you are not to add to it or take away from it.*"

The written Torah repeatedly instructs against alterations. Adding and/or subtracting from the word that God gave to Moses is strictly prohibited. Yet the oral law mythology is inherently plagued by a contradiction in which it is by its very nature constantly engaged in the game of altering the written Word of God.

After the opening verses in *Mishneh Torah*, Maimonides then goes on to address how Torah sheba'al peh was supposedly transmitted from Moses on down through the generations. He gives much of the usual litany, as found in the Talmud of how the oral law was transmitted.

Moses supposedly taught the oral law to a court of 70 elders, including Joshua, Elazar, and Pinchas. Joshua and various elders then taught it to other elders among the Jews, including allegedly Shmuel the Prophet who taught it to David.

Maimonides goes to great length in the Intro to describe the chain of authority beginning with Moses, connecting the Rabbis of the Talmudic era to an alleged divine revelation given at Sinai and passed down to the rabbis. Then the chain goes onward through Elijah and basically includes all the prophets of the Bible, the so-called "Great Assembly" during the time of Ezra and the Jews who returned from Babylon. It then goes on through the leaders of Pharisaic Judaism, to Yochanan ben Zakkai, and onward into the rabbinic Jewish leadership that wrote the Talmud.[89]

It is a self-attesting story with no corroboration found anywhere in the Bible or anywhere else. All of this about a secret law given to Moses and handed down

---

[89] Maimonides, *Mishneh Torah*, Intro, verse 4-21.

through the ages sounds very alluring. It is mysterious. People love mysteries. It reads almost like a treasure map to a secret cache of gold and gems. The Intro makes you feel like you are about to discover something that is only destined to be known by the elite.

Unlike the Bible which is open to all, this is only for those who have access to the masters and are willing to take the time to learn it. The Intro to *Mishneh Torah* is nothing like the rest of the work. The Intro is a great build up to a body of knowledge that is extremely legalistic and boring. There really isn't much reason anyone would take the time to study it at great length unless they believed the myth. The myth is the essential hook, to wit, that this is the Word of God, secretly transmitted through an elite group of God's appointees. And now it's your privilege to know it...if you are willing to submit to learn from the masters who possess it.

Chiddush – The Theory of Everything:

Connected to the idea that God gave an oral law to Moses at Sinai is the issue of how it could have been transmitted to future generations. This question of transmission is extremely problematic. After all, how does a body of knowledge get accurately transmitted orally and by memory through nearly 3,500 years of history?

The idea that Moses taught it to Joshua and then from Joshua onward, is not enough to explain divine transmission. Without a divine transmission in each succeeding generation, the oral law would be nothing more than a tradition, passed on orally from one generation to the next via human teaching. In order for it to be considered as a divine revelation, however, there must be more. There must be something to explain how the future generations of rabbinic Judaism could become the heirs of an oral teaching that supposedly was given by God to Moses then divinely transmitted somehow to them.

It is a problem that can't be addressed sensibly. Yet it has to be addressed. For the theory of a divine oral law rests upon the claim that there is an unbroken chain connecting the Rabbis of later generations with the revelation at Sinai. This connection is fundamentally necessary to assert that the word of rabbis is equal in authority to that word that Moses wrote down in the Torah.

The procedure as described in the Mishna (Avot 1), which is elaborated upon by Maimonides in his Introduction to *Mishneh Torah*, does not adequately answer the question of transmission. Some rabbinic authorities do concede the point on this. They accept that rabbinic halakha is *not* necessarily the Word of God, but more likely an attempt on the part of the rabbis to adapt Jewish life as needed to an ever-changing world. After all, how could Moses have received the halakha issued by Rabbis who lived hundreds or even thousands of years after him? Could Moses have received halakha pertaining to automobiles or computers?

This problem would seem obvious enough. But those who do concede the obvious, are conceding the point that the oral Torah is a non-Torah. Because to admit that rabbinic *halakha* was not first given by God to Moses at Sinai is to admit that the whole premise of oral is false. Specifically, it is to admit that there is no oral Torah. That admission relegates the entire body of oral law to something that is at best an oral "tradition," but not an oral Torah.

As a result, the rabbis came up with a theory. It is what could be referred to as the rabbinic "theory of everything."[90] For it maintains that everything in the great body of rabbinic law (*halakha*) was somehow given first to Moses at Sinai.

So how does this "theory of everything" work? How is it that the halakhic adaptations of today can

---

[90] "Theory of Everything" is not a term used in rabbinic Judaism, but it's used here for purposes of explaining the rabbinic approach to the issue of divine transmission.

actually be the Word of God given to Moses at Sinai over three thousand years ago?

It is here that the word "*chiddush*" comes into play. *Chiddush* is something novel or new. *Chiddush* in this context is taken to mean "innovation." It is a term that appears often in rabbinic literature to describe a form of innovation that is made inside the system of the *halakha*.

It should be noted that "*chiddush*" is distinguished from "*shinuy*," which is an innovation that is more purely practical and outside tradition. That is to say, "*chiddush*" is considered to be the Word of God within the context of *Torah sheba'al peh*; whereas *shinuy* is not the Word of God, just a practical adaptation.

Within rabbinic Judaism, there are varying approaches to this idea of what is or is not a "*chiddush*" as opposed to a "*shinuy*." What is considered within *halakha*, as opposed to outside of it can vary. But in any case, since God gave the Torah to Moses at Sinai over three thousand years ago, the *chiddush* of today has to be connected to the revelation of yesterday, at Sinai.

The basic idea of the "theory of everything," is that God gave to Moses at Sinai the complete oral Torah, including the entirety of all Jewish *halakha* yet to come in the future generations. This idea of course raises some serious problems.

The logistic impossibility of such a divine conveyance at Sinai is readily apparent. Specifically, the theory claims that the entirety of every detail of observance and belief that any Jew would ever need to know was given by God to Moses at Sinai via the oral Torah. As if God conveyed to one man at Sinai not only the details of the written Torah, but also the entirety of an oral teaching replete with all *halakha* meant to cover a time period of more than three thousand years into the future.

From this point of view, the whole of the Mishnah and Talmud, for example, are seen as a manifestation in a future time of things that were already known by Moses. Furthermore, even today's rabbinic innovation is an unfoldment of what was previously revealed at Sinai to Moses. All of this is a way to try and perpetuate the claim that rabbinic *halakha* is actually the Word of God, equal (or greater) in authority than the written scriptures.

One passage from the Talmud, Megillah 19b clearly illustrates the idea of the "theory of everything":

"What is the meaning of that which is written:
'ADONAI gave me the two tablets of stone written by the finger of God. Moreover, on them were all the words

that ADONAI had spoken with you on the mountain.' (From Deut. 9:10).

This teaches that the Holy One, Blessed be He, showed Moses on the mountain all the expositions that can be derived from the words of the Torah; and all the expositions that can be derived from the words of the Scribes, the early Sages; and also all the new halakhot that the Scribes were destined to innovate in the future in addition to the laws of the Torah."[91]

The idea that future teachings of the Rabbis are to be considered as the Word of God formerly revealed to Moses at Sinai, is found repeatedly in the Talmud. That concept continues in modern rabbinic Judaism, wherein it is commonplace to find statements like this:

"Our sages tell us that "any chiddush (novel idea) which a reputable disciple will ever come up with was already given to Moses by Sinai."[92]

---

[91] Megillah 19b. See also a discussion of this in the article by Yanki Tauber, "The Divinity of Torah," footnote 8. https://www.chabad.org/therebbe/article_cdo/aid/2619825/jewish/1-The-Divinity-of-Torah.htm#footnote8a2619825. Yanki Tauber is a Hasidic scholar, writer, and editor who served as chief content editor of Chabad.org from 1999-2013.

[92] Naftali Silberberg, "How is the Torah Interpreted," https://www.chabad.org/library/article_cdo/aid/819698/jewish/How-Is-the-Torah-Interpreted.htm.

There is another glaring example of the "theory of everything" found in the Talmud at Menachot 29b. As one prominent modern-day rabbinic commentator, Yanki Tauber, stated in reference to Menachot 29b:

"The idea that teachings expounded by later sages are also the word of G-d is illustrated by the following Talmudic account:"[93]

In support, Tauber then quotes and explains Menachot 29b, a portion of the Talmud that gives an account in which Moses was supposedly told by God about Rabbi Akiva, who lived over one thousand years later. Moses was then taken by the Lord and transported forward in time, into a class being taught by Akiva. Moses was at first confused, but then suddenly realized that Akiva was teaching something which would be given to Moses by God at Sinai.

"When Moses ascended on high, he found G-d attaching crowns to the letters of the Torah. Said Moses to G-d: 'Master of the world! Why have You need for these?'

---

[93] See the article: "The Torah Expositions of the Sages, Extraction or Innovation," by Yanki Tauber. https://www.chabad.org/therebbe/article_cdo/aid/2625328/jewish/6-The-Torah-Expositions-of-the-Sages-Extraction-or-Innovation.htm .

Said G-d to him: 'There will be a man some generations hence, whose name is Akiva the son of Joseph, and he will expound mounds upon mounds of laws from each and every tittle.'

Said Moses: 'Master of the world, show him to me.'

Moses was sitting behind eight rows (of R. Akiva's disciples) but he did not understand what they were saying, and he was despondent. Until they reached one teaching, and R. Akiva's disciples said to him, 'Master, from where do you know this?'

Said R. Akiva to them, 'It is the law given to Moses at Sinai.' And Moses' mind was eased."[94]

Like many passages from the Talmud which give accounts of Bible figures regarding circumstances nowhere mentioned in the Bible (like Moses sees God attaching crowns to the letters of the Torah), this sounds more like the stuff of mythological legends – because that's exactly what it is.

---

[94] Menachot 29b.

Stare Decisis:

The Torah in Deut. 17:8-13 sets up the Priests and Levites as a sort of judicial body for interpreting the written law. Courts are necessary in every society in order to interpret the law of the land and rightly apply it to the infinitude of diverse situations that might arise.

The law which God gave to Moses anticipated that "matters of controversy" would arise which would necessitate judicial oversight to determine how the Word of God is to be interpreted and applied. Judicial responsibility is not to change the law, but to implement it. Yet, by its very nature, the result of decisions made by judges or a judicial body is to set precedent.

To illustrate by comparison to the secular law, the principle of judicial precedent is called "stare decisis," which means literally "to stand by what was decided." The legal systems of one-third of the world, including the United States and Great Britain, for example, are "common law" systems. The common law is the body of judicial precedent set by courts interpreting and applying statutory law. At the heart of all common law systems is the idea of ensuring through stare decisis that similar facts will yield similar results.

The power of courts to enact binding legal precedent via the principle of stare decisis which inheres in case law can cause problems when judges become too active. In theory, the duty of a secular court in a common law society is the same duty as the judiciary contemplated by Deut. 17:8-13. In all likelihood, the common law system developed by looking first to the judicial precepts found in the Bible.

In either context – secular or biblical – a court in theory is expected to interpret and apply the law of the land, not to make up the law out of the clear blue. In that sense, it is the written law – given by the Legislature in a secular system or given by God in a biblical society – which is to be viewed and approached as the primary authority. The judges are to apply the law, not make it up on their own. In so doing, stare decisis operates to make the law applicable to similar situations.

Simply put, when judges deviate from the written law and start making law according to their own beliefs and values, things get out of order. As a result of unbridled judicial activism, a secular society is ripped apart at the seams.

There is a perfect parallel to rabbinic Judaism here. Because when it comes to the written Bible, judges who see their role not as interpreting and applying the written word, but as adding to or even superseding what is written, open the door to calamity and disorder among the people it serves.

Therefore, stare decisis as a precept is contemplated by the Scriptures, but not in a manner which in any way alters the written Word of God. This explains why the Torah is so clear on that particular issue. The Bible was thus given by God to Israel, and eventually to all mankind, with the clear and unequivocal instruction that it shall never be added to, subtracted from, or changed in any way.[95]

The precedent-setting authority of judges per Deut. 17:8-13 who are charged with the duty to rightly divide and implement the Word of God is a high calling indeed. This is why the judge appointed per the Torah must be a wise and honorable person, who can be impartial in judgment, and cannot be influenced by gifts or the expectation of personal gain from his decision-making.[96] A judge who will ignore the written word and instead impose his or her own values and judgments, irrespective of the plain meaning of the law, will bring chaos upon the land.[97] The best example of this kind of catastrophe is when Yeshua stood before the Sanhedrin and was rejected as the Messiah.

The glaring example from the modern secular world of the danger of judicial activism is *Roe v. Wade.*[98]

---

[95] Deut. 4:2, Deut. 12:32, Rev. 22:18.
[96] Deut. 16:19.
[97] Deut. 16:20.
[98] *Roe v. Wade,* 410 U.S. 113 (1973).

As discussed previously, the judges in *Roe* engaged in the legal hoopla of judicial activism by applying the unwarranted search and seizure principles of the Fourth amendment of the U.S. Constitution to construe what they felt ought to be the law of the land, even though it was not the law of the land.

The right of privacy and freedom from government intrusion such as what is set forth by the 4th amendment to the U.S. Constitution is indeed a great principle of a virtuous society. However, the right of a woman to terminate pregnancy via an abortion is in no way related to that constitutional provision. Such a right could of course be established by the U.S. Congress via the passage of statutory law. The elected representatives of a democratic Republic in a bicameral legislature such as the U.S. are there to serve for that very purpose of enacting laws.

However, no such law was passed. Instead, the great plague of abortion has come upon the land of the United States via the ruling of a liberal court which engaged in judicial activism. The *Roe* court changed the law of the land by second guessing the written law, and thereby imposing their own values on the people which the judges were appointed to serve. What happened in *Roe* is a great example of the dangers of judges who think themselves vested with authority to make law, independent of the written law itself.

In rabbinic Judaism we can see a similar problem. The establishment of rabbinic *halakha* is approached in some ways similar to the principle of stare decisis. However, there is also the clear belief that the role of the Rabbis is not just to interpret the written "law" but to engage in making law of their own. The Rabbis historically have presumed upon themselves the authority to make law, oftentimes completely irrespective of the Scriptures. Accordingly, rabbinic-made religious law (*halakha*) is not simply the result of construing the Scriptures; but, rather, it is often completely unrelated to Scripture at all. Rabbinic *halakha*, therefore, is not an interpretation of the existing law given by God (the Scriptures); but, instead, it is an "*ab initio*" (from the beginning) kind of action. That is to say, it is without any connection to the Scriptures, but it is a body of law unto itself.

Of course, from their own point of view, the Rabbis are acting with the presumption of having a kind of authority to make rulings and to set binding legal precedent for the Jewish people through *halakha* which is on par with the written Torah. Rabbinic *halakha*, in this manner, is treated as being "Torah", just as if it is the Word of God.

However, due to the changing conditions in which Jews have lived and the pressing need to adapt, a sort of caveat to stare decisis was developed in rabbinic Judaism called the principle of *"hilkheta ke-vatra'ei,"* which means "the law is according to the later scholars." This was necessary because after hundreds of years, it becomes obvious that certain decisions and opinions no longer make sense in a changing world.

The idea of *hilkheta ke-vatra'ei*, therefore, was to enact a new rabbinic law which proclaims that from now on the old rabbinic law is not binding to the extent that it conflicts with the new rabbinic law. Even though we had previously said that the older law was binding, we now say that from here on in, the new law takes precedent over the old.

It's a way of "undoing" the immovable effect of prior decisions as would otherwise be required due to the idea that those decisions are "Torah." Decisions that no longer make sense are thus undone by later decisions, but in a way that makes the new rabbinic decisions immovable. It's a sort of reverse stare decisis. Simply put, it gives the Rabbis exclusive power to say what is not the Word of God and what is.

That is how it is possible, in that paradigm of jurisprudence, that something which was once the Word of God according to the Rabbis, now no longer is. It is accomplished thru *hilkheta ke-vatra'ei*. Accordingly, the word of the Rabbis is treated as primary authority not only as compared to the express meaning of the written Scriptures given by God to Moses and the Prophets, but even as compared to the *"Torah sheba'al peh"* or oral law as once proclaimed by the oracles of their own community, the rabbinic voices of yesteryear.

More specifically, in rabbinic Judaism, the rule of *hilkheta ke-vatra'ei* holds that until a certain time toward the end of the Fourth Century CE, the *halakha* was to be decided according to the views of the earlier scholars; but from that time onward, the halakhic opinions of post-talmudic scholars prevail over the contrary opinions of a previous generation.[99]

Ironically, this precept of *hilkheta ke-vatra'ei* itself is a legal construct created by later rabbis. A law which empowers those who created it to say that the prior law, though once to be considered "oral Torah" is no longer the Torah at all.

In the best sense, *hilkheta ke-vatra'ei* can be approached as a way of hitting the "reset" button on a system of antiquated and often irrelevant judicial

---

[99] David E.Y. Sarna, *Supreme Court Justice Elana Kagan, Jewish Law and the Principle of Binding Precedent*, Aug. 5th, 2010: https://www.tabletmag.com/jewish-news-and-politics/41654/law-practice ;

See also: Menachem Elon, *Jewish Law: History, Sources, and Principles*.

precedent. This would allow for some change among the Jewish people as necessitated by the need to adapt. Indeed, a culture such as the Jewish people, which continues for centuries, through exile and persecution, certainly will find it necessary to grow and change and even transform through the ages. The Word of God, however, never changes.

Tradition and culture by their very nature are meant to be adaptable and changeable. However, God's word is another matter. It is immutable and constant. Thus, a judicial system which fails from the outset to rightly identify what is and what is not God's immovable, unalterable word, is doomed to make key decisions that conflict with God's unalterable word.

Judicial Authority:

The authority to say what is and is not the Word of God is a kind of authority which is "judicial" by nature. The nature and scope of rabbinic authority is typically seen within rabbinic Judaism as being connected to the judiciary referenced in Deut. 17:8-13. The idea of a divine oral law given by God to the Rabbis is connected to the claim that the Rabbis have a sort of "judicial" authority conferred by the Torah as referenced by that scriptural passage.

The validity of that claim to be sitting as judges over the people is questionable on many grounds. That particular Scripture, Deut. 17:8-13 states:

> *"Suppose a matter arises that is too hard for you to judge—over bloodshed, legal claims or assault— matters of controversy within your gates. Then you should go up to the place ADONAI your God chooses, and come to the Levitical kohanim and the judge in charge at that time. And you will inquire, and they will tell you the sentence of judgment. You are to act according to the sentence they tell you from that place ADONAI chooses, and take care to do all that they instruct you. You are to act according to the instruction they teach you and the judgment they tell you—you must not turn aside from the sentence they tell you, to the right or to the left. The man who acts presumptuously by not listening to the kohen who stands to serve there before ADONAI your God, or to the judge, that man must die. So you are to purge the evil from Israel. Then all the people will hear and be afraid, and not act presumptuously again."*

The Levites, particularly the Kohanim, were uniquely called and chosen to teach and implement the law of God in the land.[100] Yet, from the time of the

---

[100] Deut. 33:10: *"They will teach Jacob Your judgments and Israel Your*

Pharisees, to the Talmudic era, and through every succeeding generation afterwards, the leading rabbis have not necessarily been Priests and/or even Levites. In the post-Temple era, Rabbinic Jewish leadership has positioned itself in the role of the Levitical priesthood, yet rabbinic Jewish leadership has no valid claim to that position among the Jews.

Whether or not such a judiciary can even exist in the post-Temple era is questionable. There clearly is no basis in Torah for a non-Levitical body of leaders to be that judiciary. This fact in and of itself calls into question the presumption of judicial authority claimed by the Rabbis pursuant to Deut. 17:8-13.

In developing halakha, the rabbis have acted with the presumption of authority under Deut. 17:8-13. As stated previously, this is a claim that lacks validity. In any case, the divine oral law claim is based on the idea that rabbinical law is not just an interpretation of God's law, but rather the actual equivalent. This is clearly a step beyond even what was set forth for the Levitical Priests of Deut. 17:8-13.

In fact, the decision-making authority of the judges described in Deut. 17:8-13 is to take the law of God and apply it to matters of controversy. The verse emphasizes the importance of respecting the decisions

Torah."

that they make. That is not to say that the word of these *shoftim* or judges is equivalent to the Word of God.

The fact that Deut. 17:11 says: *"You are to act according to the instruction they teach you and the judgment they tell you—you must not turn aside from it,"* is meant in the context that the judges are applying the written law to everyday life. It does not mean that there is an oral Torah that they have as well, involving many laws given by God which are not recorded in what Moses wrote down in the Torah. Furthermore, it does not mean that whatever they say, whether written here in the Torah or not, is to be considered the Word of God.

That is not to say that everything the rabbis have ever said should be discarded. For one thing, from a messianic point of view, civil obedience is clearly an important biblical precept. Yeshua, for example, taught His disciples to show respect and give honor to those rabbinic leaders who sit in the "seat of Moses."

> *"Then Yeshua spoke to the crowds and to His disciples, saying, "The Torah scholars and Pharisees sit on the seat of Moses. So whatever they tell you, do and observe. But don't do what they do; for what they say, they do not do."*[101]

---

[101] Mat. 23:1–3.

From a standpoint of civil obedience, the New Testament teaches repeatedly that respect for the law of the land and obedience to civil authority is an important Bible precept. It is important even as applied to Roman rulers.[102] But it doesn't mean what the Roman Emperors, Procurators, etc. say is the Word of God. Nor did Yeshua mean that the Pharisaic leaders who sit in "the seat of Moses" are necessarily stating the Word of God. There is no endorsement of the rabbinic oral law mythology meant by Yeshua's admonition to show respect for them.

Moreover, civil obedience to the rabbinic authorities has its limitations. For example, when the disciples of Yeshua were ordered by the rabbinic leaders not to preach the gospel of Yeshua anymore, they refused. They went right on preaching it. Acts 4:18-20:

> "So they called them in and ordered them not to speak or teach at all in the name of Yeshua. But Peter and John replied, "Whether it is right in the sight of God to listen to you rather than to God, you decide. For we cannot stop speaking about what we have seen and heard."

---

[102] Rom. 13:1-7, 1 Pet. 2:13-17, Mat. 22:21.

As messianic Jews grew and multiplied in the land of Israel, following the instruction of Yeshua, in respect to rabbinic Jewish leaders they gave honor where honor was due. This was not a revolution in the classic sense. Yeshua told His followers to render unto Caesar what was Caesar's, and unto God what was God's.[103]

Accordingly, the messianic Jews meant no disrespect to prevailing rabbinic leadership, but they refused to acknowledge instructions from the rabbis which plainly contradicted the Word of God. The divide between messianic Jews and rabbinic leadership was clear. Clearly at first, many messianic Jews still worshipped in the Temple and moved about among the mainstream Jewish community. But eventually after the fall of the Temple, they were put out of the synagogues and the Jewish communities as the Pharisaic leaders rose to a monopoly of power.

The dividing line was drawn over the matter of judicial authority. That is, the authority to say what is and is not the Word of God. Messianic Jews from the outset rejected the premise of Torah sheba'al peh (oral Torah), and this has placed them at odds with the rabbinic community right up to this day.

---

[103] Mark 12:17.

The Jewish Courts:

Although the Torah ordains a kind of court system, historically, there isn't much record regarding the operation or the rulings of the Jewish courts. In that regard, the New Testament is a very informative historical document concerning the Sanhedrin. The Sanhedrin is mentioned repeatedly in the New Testament. It met to discuss what to do about Yeshua as He rose to great fame among the Jewish people; and also was the body before which Yeshua was tried.[104] Moreover, the Apostles of Yeshua had various encounters with the Sanhedrin as described in the book of Acts. [105]

During the time of Yeshua, the Sanhedrin is mentioned twenty-two times in the New Testament as the High Court of the Jewish people in the land. Sanhedrin comes from the Greek word "synhedrion" meaning "sitting together." The Sanhedrin consisted of seventy-one men and met in a Chamber on the grounds of the Temple in Jerusalem. Smaller courts of either twenty-three, or of three, were used to judge cases of lesser importance.

The earliest record of the Sanhedrin is from 57 BCE. A Sanhedrin continued to function in various

---

[104] Mark 14:55, and 15:1.
[105] Acts 5:21–41; and Acts 22:30 and 23:1.

locations after the Second Temple period. It moved around from Yavneh to Usha, and various locations in the Southern Galilee, eventually settling in Tiberius. The last meeting of the Sanhedrin was in 425 CE.

Although the scriptural basis is provided in the Torah (Deut. 17:8-13) for the creation of something like a judicial system under Priestly and Levitical authority, it is not clear how that worked exactly. The first actual historical evidence of the Sanhedrin (other than the Talmud and later rabbinical writings) appears no earlier than the First Century BCE, during the Hasmonean era of the Second Temple. Therefore, little is known about how the Torah-based Jewish court system actually functioned, let alone the specifics of cases which they may have adjudicated.

The lack of any historical record of a Jewish court prior to the Sanhedrin is an important fact, because judicial precedent is impossible to establish when there is no record of a court system, let alone actual documents of decisions made. Trying to establish what is or is not precedent without documentary proof isn't possible. It leaves us entirely to the nebulous, unreliable speculation of an oral tradition which was created mainly by non-levitical religious leaders with a political agenda to supplant the scriptural role of the Levitical Priesthood as established under Deut. 17:8-13.

The rabbinic writings, for example, beginning with the Talmud, attempt to connect the rabbinic legal system of the post Second Temple era to the Jewish high court of earlier times. The Talmud draws much reference to what is called the *"Anshei knesset haGedolah"* (Men of the Great Assembly).

In that respect, Maimonides in his *Mishneh Torah* restated what was said in the Talmud, claiming that Ezra set up 120 elders and called it the *Anshei Knesset haGedolah*.[106] This great assembly is described by the Rabbis as being part of the chain of commission of the Oral Torah. As stated in the Talmud, regarding transmission of the oral Torah, Pirkei Avot 1:1 :

> *"Moshe received the Torah from Sinai and transmitted it to Yehoshua, and Yehoshua to the Elders, and the Elders to the Prophets, and the Prophets transmitted it to the **Men of the Great Assembly**."*

The idea of an *Anshei Knesset haGedolah*, or men of the Great Assembly, is somewhat sketchy. While it certainly may have existed, that doesn't mean it was the repository of a divinely transmitted oral Torah. The supposed Great Assembly is not clearly found either in the Bible or in any plain historical or archeological

---

[106] Maimonides, *Mishneh Torah*, Introduction, verse 7.

record. The Talmud and later rabbinic writings are the main source for it. They attempt to link it with the narrative in Nehemiah 8-10 regarding the return of Jewish elders from exile. But that is a stretch.

In any case, considering the motive of the rabbis to connect themselves in some way to the authority of the Jewish court system, obviously the veracity of what the Talmud says about the Great Assembly cannot be relied upon. However, it certainly is reasonable to believe that such a thing as the Great Assembly may have existed. Indeed, Ezra might have organized a Jewish court in the Second Temple period consisting of elders among the returnees from Babylon. After all, as stated previously, the Torah ordains the establishment of a judiciary among the people Israel, so clearly there was a court system ordained by the Torah. It is entirely possible and probable that Ezra and/or other leaders might have set something up when the Jews returned to rebuild the Temple.

The problem is that there are no records showing what was said or done by Jewish courts prior to that first mention of the Sanhedrin, during the Hasmonean era, in the First Century BCE. Everything said about the *Anshei Knesset haGedolah* otherwise comes from a later era, beginning when the Talmud was written. That information is based on the speculation of alleged oral records.

To be clear, this is not a denial that something like the Great Assembly existed. Not only is it reasonable that the *Anshei Knesset haGedolah* might have existed, but also that it might have been responsible for some of the works attributed to it. For example, the canonization of the Tanakh, is often attributed in rabbinic thought as a work of the men of the Great Assembly. That is entirely reasonable.

However, the Talmud and later the restatement of it found in the *Mishneh Torah* of Maimonides, involves many other claims connected to the Great Assembly which are intended as an extension of their mythology concerning the transmission of the supposed oral Torah. The Talmud and other rabbinic writings claim that the oral Torah was handed down through the *Anshei Knesset haGedolah*. Much of what they say, therefore, relative to the Great Assembly, is offered in conjunction with their overarching claims regarding the existence of an oral law.

For example, the Talmud ascribes the institution and formulation of Jewish benedictions and liturgical worship to the men of the Great Assembly. They claim, for example, that prayers like the Amidah, the Kiddush,

Havdala, and so forth, were formulated under Ezra's leadership by the *Anshei Knesset haGedolah.*[107]

With that approach, the liturgy of rabbinic Judaism is not just a beautiful way of bringing Jews together to engage in communal prayer, but, the liturgy is an actual revelation from God, a method of prayer delivered to Israel via the oral Torah. Accordingly, it is considered vital to pray certain prayers and to say them in a certain way and under the purview of certain leaders.

For example, the Talmud goes to great lengths to make the case how one ought to say the full *Shema* prayer.[108] The claims of the rabbis to be the heirs of a divinely revealed Jewish liturgy is just one of many such examples of how the *Anshei Knesset haGedolah* is seen as a great depository in the chain of transmission of the supposed oral Torah.

Of course, it is reasonable to believe, and could very well be true that corporate Jewish prayer life was established by some body of spiritual elders during the Second Temple period, beginning with Ezra.[109] However, as approached in orthodox Judaism, Jewish liturgy is not

---

[107] See, Ber. 33a.

[108] See: Meg. 17(b).

[109] It should be noted here that Messianic Synagogues typically use some traditional rabbinic liturgical worship in services. However, messianic Jews see Jewish liturgy as culture, but not as a divine revelation from God.

seen as a mere cultural development, but as a divine revelation. Hence, the rabbinic speculation over the *Anshei Knesset haGedolah* is always connected to the purpose of adding credibility to the claim of a divinely transmitted oral Torah. This is perpetuated today by orthodox Judaism.

Additionally, many orthodox Jews today believe that the *Anshei Knesset haGedolah* even went so far as to codify what it means to be a "Jew." As if, per the ruling of the Great Assembly, the Jews who returned to the land in Ezra's time were identified by submission and adherence to the teachings of rabbinic Judaism and the oral Torah. According to that view, a "Jew" is a person who submits to the beliefs of rabbinic Judaism.

That is why, to this day, the orthodox establishment views non-orthodox Jews as not Jewish. To them, being "Jewish" is defined by accepting the beliefs of orthodoxy. Needless to say, Theodore Herzl, the father of the Jewish state, would not fit that definition of being Jewish. The same could be said about David Ben-Gurion, and Gold Meir, and so many other Zionist Jewish leaders of our modern time who did not identify with rabbinic orthodoxy.

The oral law mythology was created by self-appointed judges, with no biblical basis for their authority, who came into judicial power in a time of great political instability. This explains how and why one of the greatest jurisprudential errors of all time was made by the Sanhedrin two thousand years ago. In spite of thousands of Jews throughout the land proclaiming Yeshua to be the Messiah, the Sanhedrin held that Yeshua is not the Messiah. That erroneous ruling has been handed down from generation to generation, right up to today among the Jewish people.

Chapter Three: The Mesorah

Oral Torah Within Messianic Judaism:

The Jewish people globally are all impacted by rabbinic doctrine and practice. We can't get away from it completely even if we wanted to. The Talmud and other writings of the rabbis, which are essential to rabbinic Judaism, are not necessarily dismissed outright by Messianic Jews. We do not label all rabbinic writings as "evil" or anything like that.

Messianic Jews generally respect and honor the wisdom of the sages of old. We have no agenda to remove from our midst all things having to do with rabbinic Judaism. Some Messianic Jews study the writings of the Rabbis, and we are not necessarily opposed to it. However, the Messianic Jewish approach to rabbinic Judaism must necessarily have certain limitations.

In particular, the key problem with the oral Torah is that it claims to be the Word of God. That is not a collateral or minor issue within the collection of rabbinic teaching of which the oral Law is constituted. It is the very foundation stone upon which the house of rabbinic Judaism is built.

Messianic Jews reject any authority other than the written Scriptures as the Word of God. The written Scriptures found in the Bible—both Tanakh and New Covenant—are the only infallible and authoritative Word of God that mankind has. To be clear, any claim involving a divine oral law would be violative of the statement of faith of the IAMCS and of the MJAA.[110] The UMJC has a similar statement, stating that the Scriptures are "of supreme and final authority in all matters of faith and practice." [111]

In fact, the Messianic Jewish movement in the mainstream considers completely unacceptable the idea of a divine oral Torah. The Christian world takes a similar view. It is essential to New Covenant faith that

[110] The MJAA and IAMCS Statement of Faith state: "THE BIBLE" states: "That the BIBLE, consisting of the Tenach (Holy Scriptures) and the later writings commonly known as the B'rit Hadasha (New Covenant), is the only infallible and authoritative Word of God. We recognize its divine inspiration and accept its teachings as our final authority in all matters of faith and practice (Deut. 6:4-9; Prov. 3:1-6; Ps. 119:89, 105; Isa. 48:12-16; Rom. 8:14-17; II Tim. 2:15, 3:16-17)." See: https://iamcs.org/about-us/belief.

[111] https://www.umjc.org/statement-of-faith

the Bible is the Word of God. After all, if there were such a thing as a divine oral Torah, there would be no legitimate claim to the authority of written Scripture, upon which faith in Yeshua is based.

Nevertheless, oddly enough, over the last fifty years of the modern Messianic Jewish movement, occasionally there are certain individuals who seek to import into the movement the orthodox belief and approach to Torah, including the belief in a divine oral Torah. As absurd as this may seem on its face, there has been a recent upsurge in this phenomenon.

While rabbinic Judaism clearly has an influence upon the culture of Messianic Judaism, the rabbinic claim to be the heirs of a divine oral law is not only untrue, but it creates a contradiction that can't be reconciled with the messianic faith. Believers in Yeshua who take up that mantle and try to import it into the body of the Messiah are entering into a bizarre game that is wrought with hypocrisy. Oral law theology runs counter to the basic biblical faith in Messiah Yeshua.

After all, it is the orthodox rabbinic authority which says Yeshua is *not* the Messiah. Though the Scriptures bear witness that Yeshua *is* Messiah, it is the oral Torah upon which the Rabbis base their claim that He is not the Messiah. To the extent that the Scriptures plainly demonstrate that Yeshua is indeed the Messiah, oral Torah gives the rabbis a basis for explaining it away.

There is no way to harmonize oral Torah theology with faith in Yeshua. It is clearly and unequivocally a doctrine that rejects Yeshua, as not only the Bible demonstrates, but also the writings of the rabbis do boldly declare that Yeshua is not Messiah. One cannot accept the doctrinal premise of oral Torah, i.e. that it was given by God to Moses at Sinai and transmitted to the generations of rabbinic elders, but then pick through it and say "all this stuff about Yeshua not being the Messiah has to be thrown out." If God gave it at Sinai, it can't be thrown out.

The Rabbis have maintained the posture of rejecting Yeshua for nearly two millennia, and all the while maintaining that the oral Torah gives them the authority to say so on behalf of all Israel. Which it does. But only if one accepts its premise.

As soon as one accepts oral Torah as being of divine nature, that is a consensual agreement that the rabbi's rejection of Yeshua must be correct because it is from God. After all, if God gave Moses the future halakha at Sinai, surely God also gave Moses the ruling of the Sanhedrin which rejected Yeshua, along with all future halakha that has maintained that rejection for the last two millennia.

For people who claim to believe Yeshua is Messiah, one can only wonder why they are seeking to validate the premise upon which the orthodox rabbinic community claims that Yeshua is *not* the Messiah. For those of us from among the Jews and among the Gentiles, who wait for Messiah's return, and share the hope, expressed by Sha'ul to the Romans, *"so shall all Israel be saved,"*[112] we know that one of the great obstacles is that oral law myth created by rabbinic Judaism. It is acceptance of that myth which gives the Rabbis authority to hold the people in blindness and darkness as to the identity of Messiah. They presume to have power to say who is the Messiah, even when the Spirit of the Lord, and the Holy Scriptures already testify to it – Yeshua hu HaMashiach! Yeshua is the Messiah.

Every Jew who accepts Yeshua as Messiah inevitably hears "but the Rabbis say Yeshua can't be the Messiah!" Indeed, the Rabbis say Yeshua is not the Messiah. But the Scriptures declare the truth that He is Messiah. The Rabbis say they are the ones who have authority to say who is the Messiah. How absurd for believers in Yeshua to affirm the rabbinic claim by affirming the means from which they claim to have that authority – the oral Torah.

---

[112] Rom. 11:26.

Messing Around with the Mesorah:

It is inherently contradictory, therefore, for believers in Yeshua to advocate a belief in the divine oral Torah claim of rabbinic Judaism. Yet, incredible as it may seem, there are some today who do so. There are varied approaches to it. Recently, one of the more prominent teachings of this kind refers to itself as the "mesorah."

The term "mesorah" literally means "transmission." Although scarcely found in orthodox rabbinic theology, sometimes it can be found as a reference to the transmission of oral Torah from Moses at Sinai to future generations through the development of halakha.[113] Generally, however, the label "mesorah" is a rarity in orthodox circles. The term is mainly being used today by those who seek to import the oral Torah teaching into the context of messianic faith. Hence, for our purposes here, the use of the term "mesorah" is hereinafter meant in reference to the "messianic" version of it.

[113] See, e.g.: Immanuel Bernstein: "Preserving our Mesorah in Changing Times," https://jewishaction.com/religion/preserving_our_mesorah_a_symposium2/ ; and Michael Rosensweig, "Mesorah as Halachic Source and Sensibility," https://jewishaction.com/religion/mesorah_as_halachic_source_and_sensibility/

In that regard, the messianic "mesorah" teaching affirms the orthodox belief in two Torahs. In fact, strange as it may seem, the mesorah teachers tell messianic believers to accept all the same litany of orthodox rabbinic Judaism in regard to the claim that there is a Torah *shebichtav* and Torah *sheba'al peh*, a written law and oral law. Both were allegedly given directly by God to Moses at Sinai.

Those messianic mesorah teachers affirm orthodox belief that the oral version of Torah was supposedly given by God to Moses at Sinai. They refer as authority to the Pirkei Avot, and all that is restated by Maimonides in *Mishneh Torah* concerning the transmission of oral Torah from Moses to Joshua and so forth, thru the *Anshei Knesset haGedolah*, and onward to the Rabbis of the Talmud and beyond.

Just like the orthodox, mesorah teachers make a big point about the claim that no one can understand the written Scriptures without the oral. They stress the need, therefore, to learn the Talmud, as well as the teachings of the rabbinic masters, such as Rashi, Rambam, and so forth. They make no effort to downplay the fact that they see rabbinic teaching as essential. They do not dispute and seem to confirm the belief that *halakha* is to be considered at least equal, if not greater, in authority than the written word. A key difference, however, when it comes to the issue of divine transmission, they add to the chain of those holy recipients of the divine oral Torah one key party—themselves.

The idea of mesorah teachers suggesting to the public that they are the messianic "ark-bearers" of the oral Torah of rabbinic Judaism is patently absurd. It is, after all, an anti-Yeshua teaching by its very nature. But this claim seems to be necessary as a way of addressing the key problem for messianic believers who go after this mesorah teaching. The problem is that Yeshua is rejected by the Talmud and its progeny of rabbis through the ages. Hence, mesorah teachers seem to be suggesting that they are the end-time resolution of this problem.

But rabbinic halakha from the Talmudic period right up to today has held that Yeshua is not the Messiah. If Yeshua is Messiah then it's game over for orthodox rabbinic Judaism. Because if He is Messiah, then the whole halakhic ship is sunk. Halakha would become at best advisory, but clearly not a revelation from God to Moses. It is to concede that halakha is not Torah, but non-Torah.

Mesorah teachers would like to be seen as modern-day heirs of the Torah *sheba'al peh*, which formerly was transmitted by the orthodox rabbinic establishment, but now has been transmitted by God to these mesorah teachers who claim to be representatives of Yeshua. It's a preposterous claim. But, sadly, there are people out there, mostly non-Jewish, who come into it unawares. They are not well-acquainted with Jewish history or culture and are not informed of what they are getting into. Some also might not realize that such a thing is anathema to mainstream messianic Jewish teaching.

The Pre-Sinai Oral Torah:

One key characteristic of the mesorah teaching that is somewhat different than the usual orthodox approach, is they emphasize the belief that the oral law was also given by God to the Patriarchs. The mesorah teaching claims that Abraham and the other two Patriarchs received the oral Torah, which was later imparted in full to Moses at Sinai in both oral and written form. Because of this supposed pre-Sinai revelation of the oral Torah, including the halakha that goes with it, mesorah teaching claims that Abraham, Isaac and Jacob were keeping the Torah even before it was given to Moses. For the most part, this approach goes even further than most in orthodox Judaism.[114]

---

[114] The idea of the Patriarchs receiving and observing halakha via

Abraham is the father of the household of God for Jew and non-Jew alike.[115] At various times, God spoke to Abraham, and Abraham obeyed God. The fact that the Lord spoke to Abraham is not to say that He gave Abraham an oral Torah. Genesis 26:5, however, is taken out of context and relied upon by mesorah teachers who try to make that claim.[116]

Simply put, what set Abraham apart in his generation was faith in God. Both Old and New Testament state: *"Abraham believed God and it was credited to him as righteousness."*[117] But a sincere biblical faith in Messiah Yeshua requires reliance upon the written Scriptures as authority. A Bible-based faith cannot therefore be maintained within the context of a belief that there is also an oral Torah. This is because the oral Torah requires faith in those who quite specifically say in their "oral Torah" that Yeshua is not Messiah.

---

some kind of a pre-Sinai revelation from God is not emphasized nor universally endorsed in the Orthodox Rabbinic camp. But it is not unheard of either. Some claim that Abraham kept only the seven Noachide laws, others see Abraham going a lot further in his Torah observance. The Talmud, Yoma 28b, records a discussion of varying of views on this.

[115] Gal. 3:29 – *"And if you belong to Messiah, then you are Abraham's seed—heirs according to the promise."*

[116] Gen. 26:5 – *"Because that Abraham obeyed my voice, and kept my charge, my commandments, my statutes, and my laws."*

[117] Rom. 4:3, Gen. 15:6 and Gal. 3:61.

There are different manners of expressions, but a sincere follower of Yeshua inevitably belongs to a faith that is a "Bible-faith." He or she appreciates knowledge, education, wisdom, etc. that might be found in other resources, but recognizes nonetheless, that the written Bible is the only authoritative Word of God.

Contrarily, the follower of the mesorah teaching inevitably finds himself or herself entangled in a web which necessitates the affirmation of something *other than* the Bible as *also* the Word of God. That is deeply problematic considering that the thing which must be confirmed is a massive collection of rabbinic teaching which emphatically and plainly maintains that Messiah has not yet come, and that Yeshua was a false prophet.

That is not to say that Talmud and other key rabbinic works are inherently evil. Nor does it mean that people should never study rabbinic literature. There is value in studying rabbinic wisdom and it may be worthwhile for some who have that interest. But it is completely unnecessary for the fullness of Life in Messiah and/or for maintaining a healthy messianic faith.

When non-Jews become engrossed and enamored with rabbinic studies, this often seems to be particularly troublesome. This is not to say that non-Jews should never study Talmud or anything like that. However, generally speaking, non-Jewish fascination with orthodox rabbinism always seems to be a lethal concoction. It is usually accompanied by a desire to prove oneself on a higher spiritual level than average non-Jewish believer in Yeshua and/or to prove oneself Jewish. It is elementary that in the body of Messiah, being Jewish or non-Jewish is not the issue. As Sha'ul wrote in Rom. 3:23-24:

> *"For there is no distinction, for all have sinned and fall short of the glory of God. They are set right as a gift of His grace, through the redemption that is in Messiah Yeshua."*

Yet for some, being redeemed by God's grace, washed clean by the blood of the Lamb, is somehow not enough for righteousness. Somehow, they feel that one must additionally delve into the teachings of the orthodox rabbis to learn how to walk with God according to correct *halakha*.

To embrace orthodox rabbinic halakha as authoritative is to endorse the anti-Yeshua protocol of that same body of rabbinic thinking which rejects Yeshua. A person who accepts the oral Torah mythology is inevitably placing themselves in conflict with the basic foundational principles of messianic faith, beginning with the principle that Yeshua is the Lamb slain for the sins of the world.

After all, the rabbinic writings expressly condemn any idea suggesting that someone could die for our sins. The devoted student of the "oral Torah" is given a plethora of reasons why atonement through the shed blood of Messiah violates "Torah." And this same teaching is being imported into the messianic movement under the label "mesorah," as if it somehow is the fulfillment of messianic faith. The fact is that oral Torah is unbiblical. So, too, is oral Torah with the twist that it now somehow applies to messianic life.

Yeshua the Pharisee:

One of the common claims of the promoters of mesorah is that the ministry of Yeshua is somehow meant to be a continuation of Pharisaic Judaism. In this skewed presentation of the "gospel," Yeshua is seen as a Pharisee. The mesorah also claims that Yeshua Himself was actually a Pharisee, along with Yochanan the Immerser, and all the *sh'lichim* (apostles), as well as the bulk of Yeshua's first *talmidim* (disciples).

In that sense, the messianic Jewish movement and calling is presented as a construct and continuation of Pharisaic Judaism. The "Yeshua the Pharisee" claim is set forth as a kind of apologetic for our alleged mandate to accept and embrace the oral Torah. After all, if Yeshua was a Pharisee, then we who today consider ourselves Yeshua's disciples, must look to Pharisaic Judaism in order to come into the fullness of what it means to be "true" and "authentic" *talmidim* of the Lord. Naturally, this approach includes adherence to the foundational belief of Pharisaic Judaism – the divinely imparted oral Torah. In this twisted paradigm, "Yeshua the Pharisee" is presented as the affirmation of the very rabbinic establishment which opposed him on account of their non-scriptural traditions, the same which he upbraided and rebuked at every turn. Indeed, the same establishment which to this day claims that Yeshua is not the Messiah.

This contradiction notwithstanding, the mesorah teacher propagates the idea of "Yeshua the Pharisee," and then typically hold himself out to the public as one who has "expertise" on Pharisaic Judaism. The level of that "expertise" is often dubious. Yet, it is a hook for those who don't know better. Therefore, in order to be a "true" follower of Yeshua, one must learn what the teacher has learned—the oral law of God. Such learning, of course, can only be acquired via the "masters," as they would like to be considered, who hold themselves out as God's appointed experts of the "complete Torah," albeit with the twist that the oral Torah is somehow congruent with life in Yeshua.

The *talmidim* of mesorah teaching, therefore, will distinguish themselves by spiritually rising above not only the unbelievers of the world, but also the masses of "ignorant" believers out there who know the Lord only in the written word but not in the oral. After all, no one can understand the written word so long as they have neglected to learn the orally transmitted "Torah." But now, we too can live the fullness of messianic life by understanding the Pharisaic wisdom found in the *Torah sheba'al peh*, that is, the oral Torah which supposedly was followed by the Apostles and the early disciples of Yeshua, and of which Yeshua Himself was the chief oracle.

As to the idea that Yeshua was a Pharisee, and that His followers too are supposed to be Pharisees, of course, nothing could be further from the truth. If Yeshua made any point at all regarding the Pharisees and their ways it was the point that He was *not* one of them. While even the dregs of society – drunkards, harlots, tax-collectors, and sinners of all kind – were capable of grasping Yeshua's transformational salvation message, the one and only people group toward which Yeshua ever used condemnatory and harsh words was the Pharisees.

This is not to discount that there were key individual members of the Pharisaic sect who became believers in Yeshua. But as a sect, no one group was more committed to opposing Yeshua then the Pharisees. And that opposition, the crux of which was based on Yeshua's non-recognition of their *halakha*, has continued onward into future generations right up to today. To suggest that Yeshua and/or Messianic Judaism was or is Pharisaic is preposterous. It flies in the face of reality and common sense.

Another feature of mesorah teaching is adherence to the orthodox belief that the condition precedent for Messiah's coming along with the promise of *Geulah* (redemption), is entirely premised on a return to Torah observance. Comparatively, in orthodox rabbinic Judaism, the idea is that we must keep Torah in order for Messiah to come. And by "keep Torah" they mean the halakha of the oral Torah, which really means submission to the rabbis who created it to begin with.

The mesorah teachers of the supposed "messianic" faith teach the same idea. Messiah won't return until people learn the mesorah and keep the halakha. This you can do only by submitting to the experts. Not to mention signing up for their course, paying the fees, and buying their materials. That may sound sarcastic, but it is factual and true. The whole point of the oral law mythology is to add force and credibility to the claims of the teacher to be a master, so that he can rule over you.

The Setting of the Stage:

Since the late 1960's and 1970's, there have been those who have tried to interject orthodox rabbinic Judaism into the context of the Messianic Jewish revival. It has been well-established over the last forty to fifty years that any of these kinds of efforts which make "Torah" the issue, never seem to lead anywhere good. Oftentimes, they give rise to controversies, factionalism, and division.

As we have seen from time to time, these certain individual persons who do arise with the intent to advocate ideas borrowed heavily from orthodox rabbinic Judaism, often are not very mature spiritually. Consequently, lacking spiritual maturity, such an individual typically seeks to be viewed in the movement as a sort of resident "Torah expert," and will in furtherance of this recognition rely heavily upon studies in orthodox Judaism which are not connected to, let alone found within the written Scriptures. Such an individual might by this pretense be able to garner the attention of an audience of followers who are interested in that niche.

In Messianic Judaism, the modern movement is blessed with an influx of devoted non-Jewish congregants who have the messianic Jewish vision. In messianic Judaism, we see Jew and non-Jew as one in Messiah Yeshua through faith, just as Sha'ul described it, together in the "olive tree."[118] Committed, faithful non-Jews who are called and who share the core vision for Israel's salvation and restoration are found in every messianic synagogue.

People who do not come from a Jewish background may not be sufficiently informed about the errors or even dangers which inhere in orthodox rabbinic Judaism. That is why there is a particular sense of urgency felt by many Messianic Rabbis to protect the non-Jewish sheep from the wolves that come into the movement targeting non-Jews with a heavily orthodox rabbinic message.

The "Torah expert" within the messianic fold typically targets an audience consisting mainly of non-Jews. Not exclusively, but mainly. This is probably attributable to the fact that Jewish people who have come to know Yeshua as Messiah, are already familiar with the errors and hypocrisy of orthodox Jewish

---

[118] Rom. 11:17-24.

theology and practice. Rejection of orthodoxy is usually a factor when Jews come to faith in Yeshua to begin with. Simply put, Jewish believers generally don't want to go back to rabbinic Judaism, but forward with a Judaism that is biblical and Messiah-centered.

The heavily orthodox type of message always seems to be not only targeted at non-Jews, but embraced by those non-Jews who suffer from identity issues. The result of submitting to these self-proclaimed Torah-experts can lead to a falling away or even outright apostasy.

Scripturally, it is apparent that Sha'ul often confronted the same kind of teaching two thousand years ago. Therefore, Sha'ul frequently found it necessary to defend the messianic faith from similar efforts by those who had gone out among the Gentiles, motivated by self-aggrandizement, teaching a message based in Torah mythology. In the very same cities and regions where the Lord had sent Sha'ul to preach the Good News, came these self-important teachers, who went out preaching not the Good News that the Apostles preached, but instead, a heavy orthodox rabbinic message. They particularly targeted the Gentiles who were coming to faith in Messiah. For example, Sha'ul enjoined Timothy to oppose those who wanted to be thought of as "Torah teachers":

"Remain on at Ephesus so that you may instruct certain men not to teach strange doctrines, nor to pay attention to myths and endless genealogies, which give rise to mere speculation rather than furthering the administration of God which is by faith."[119]

The problem with this sort of teacher about which Sha'ul warned Timothy, and the reason why they promote among the Gentiles the myths and fables of orthodox rabbinism is because they are self-important and want to be seen as "Torah Teachers." Sha'ul continues:

"For some men, straying from these things, have turned aside to fruitless discussion, wanting to be teachers of the Law, even though they do not understand either what they are saying or the matters about which they make confident assertions.[120]

Accordingly, the motive and attitude of the mesorah teacher today is essentially the same as those teachers which Sha'ul had to confront, the type who desired to be thought of as experts in the Torah. Being an expert himself, and having been raised a Pharisee, at

---

[119] 1 Tim. 1:3-4 NASB.
[120] 1 Tim. 1:6,7 NASB.

the feet of Gamaliel, Sha'ul knew what he was talking about.[121]

Hebrew Roots:

In 2014, the IAMCS published its position paper, *One Law, Two Sticks,*[122] which was a critique of the modern Hebrew Roots movement. The oral mesorah teaching is different in some ways, but in other ways it is clearly connected to the Hebrew Roots movement in that it appeals to the same sort of crowd.

As often is the case with anything having to do with "Torah" that is marketed to a mass audience by individuals or groups that refer to themselves as "messianic," inevitably, the target audience for what they call "Torah" is mainly non-Jewish. The whole matter of advocating Torah observance as a requirement is complicated, particularly when aimed at non-Jews. Typically, that kind of message appeals to people who struggle with identity issues, and who want to feel somehow that they are true "Israelites," even truer Israelites than Jewish people. Inevitably, this is where "Torah" comes in. Torah is always put out as the way

---

[121] Phil. 3:5, Acts 22:3.
[122] One Law, Two Sticks, IAMCS Steering Committee, Jan. 2014.

for a non-jew to think of himself or herself as Jewish, and moreover, even more Jewish than Jews.

Of course, the biblical messianic faith has its root in the Jewish people. The growing number of non-Jewish believers in Yeshua who see the Jewish roots of their faith is truly exciting. It is comforting and heart-warming to Jews of all backgrounds and beliefs to see non-Jews acknowledging the Jewish root of their faith. Many Jews who don't know Yeshua are provoked to salvation by this.

From one nation, came the salvation of all nations. It is clear that the one Messiah came from Israel, but also that He came for all mankind. Without regard to ethnicity nor nationality nor race, one Lord came for all. Therefore, it is fundamental that issues regarding salvation, righteousness and holiness, etc. do not depend on being Jewish or non-Jewish. Thus, Sha'ul told the non-Jewish believers among the Galatians, as they were beginning to come to faith in Messiah: "*If you let yourself be circumcised Messiah will be of no benefit to you.*"[123]

Nevertheless, teachers who advocate a heavy-handed message about Torah observance do typically aim for a non-Jewish audience. And they seem to connect with those who are dissatisfied with basic new

---

[123] Gal. 5:2.

covenant faith. Frequently, their message also attracts individuals with sketchy claims having to do with Jewish ancestry,[124] who feel that being thought of as "Jewish" is somehow necessary for them.

Oftentimes, this kind of audience enjoys hearing flagrant condemnation toward the Gentile church on account of their lack of "Torah" and that sort of thing. At other times, they are displeased with messianic Jews too, on account of our approach to what they call "Torah," because we supposedly aren't observant enough. In the case of the mesorah, for example, messianic Jews are criticized as falling short, because we don't believe in an oral Torah, nor embrace rabbinic *halakha* as authoritative.

As the IAMCS expressed in 2014 in the Preface to *One Law, Two Sticks*:

"We, as Messianic Jewish leaders, have become increasingly concerned that there are a growing number of individuals and groups today promoting the idea that all the world's believers in the Messiah – Jewish and Gentile alike – ought to be keeping the Torah, particularly the Shabbat, the feasts, and kosher diet."

---

[124] This is not in any way to disparage those with legitimate, verifiable ancestry, for whatever value it may be to them.

The new thing today – the mesorah – suggests that all the world's believers ought to be learning the oral Torah and practicing the halakha as dictated by the Rabbis. After all, no one can understand Scripture without the oral Law, and moreover, those who sign up for yeshiva classes, pay the fees, and start learning oral Torah, will hasten the day of Yeshua's return by doing so.

Oftentimes, what is taught by the mesorah teacher is so fundamentally out of sync with basic messianic Jewish belief and practice, that they would not even qualify for ordination by a reputable messianic Jewish organization for that matter. Unfortunately, however, anybody anywhere can call themselves "messianic" or a "messianic Rabbi," if they so choose. This creates some confusion as to what messianic Jews actually believe (which is why a publication like this becomes necessary).

Before there was anything called a "Hebrew Roots" movement, there was the Two-house movement. It was also called Ephraimite and Messianic Israelite. In 1999 the International Messianic Jewish Alliance published *the Ephraimite Error,* exposing the Two-house movement as a cult of non-Jews claiming to be Jews. After that, proponents of Two-house theology began referring to themselves instead as Hebrew Roots. It was the same teaching, aimed at the same audience, only under a different name.

Since the publication of the IAMCS paper *One Law, Two Sticks* in 2014,[125] many Hebrew Roots teachers now gravitate away from the term "Hebrew Roots." Many opt to call themselves "messianic" or even "messianic Rabbis." They even call their ministries "messianic" instead of "Hebrew Roots." It's a new twist on an old message, aimed at the same audience – non-Jewish people who want to be thought of as Jewish through Torah-observance.

The Hebrew roots movement clearly set the stage and gave an audience to the new thing aimed at the same audience – the mesorah.

The New Thing – the Mesorah:

As with the Two-House and the Hebrew Roots movement, the mesorah teaching is characterized by fascination with the "Torah." Mesorah is different, however, in that it is a message that advocates not only observance of written Torah, but also the oral Torah of orthodox Judaism.

---

[125] *One Law, Two Sticks*, A Critical Look at the Hebrew Roots Movement, IAMCS 2014. See: https://iamcs.org/about-us/position-papers

In any case, just like the Two-House and Hebrew Roots movement, the mesorah has the potential to be divisive within Messianic Judaism, particularly among non-Jewish people who aren't otherwise acquainted with rabbinic Judaism. As stated previously, that is the reason for this publication, to point out the error so that the public can be informed as to the truth.

Since the normative messianic Jewish mainstream does not recognize oral Torah or a divine oral Law of any form, those within the messianic Jewish movement who might be tempted to embrace mesorah teaching will inevitably find themselves at odds with mainstream teaching. Accordingly, mesorah teaching is not only a message that is fundamentally unscriptural, but potentially divisive as well. Although messianic Rabbis do teach and practice certain aspects of Jewish culture and tradition as handed down by rabbinic Judaism, there are limits to it. Indeed, messianic Rabbis do not teach the oral Torah because messianic Rabbis don't believe there is such a thing.

Mesorah teachers, therefore, often call into question the messianic Jewish movement's validity on account of its non-endorsement of a divine oral Torah. That divisive element is very much a part of the mesorah message. That makes it more appealing to the fanatics among the Hebrew roots crowd, and also creates potential for division among the misinformed within the normative messianic Jewish synagogue.

Use of Multi-Media technology:

Today's technology has changed the game for people who teach the Scriptures. An engaging personality with even a semblance of expertise regarding multi-media marketing can potentially gather an audience on the internet. The ability to attract a crowd is not based on message content. It is far more based on format and personality. This is particularly true in regard to the use of the powerful medium of livestream video technology.

Video livestream today is a medium which is zero to low budget and is available to anyone. In order to reach the masses with a particular teaching, however aberrant, no longer is it necessary to acquire the great resources once needed to produce television shows, nor tailor them to be fit for standards of religious broadcasting. Nor does a teacher need to be trained, mentored, licensed and ordained, nor in a position of accountability to any major umbrella organization.

In this modern era, a Yeshiva-like study program can be embarked upon by just about anyone who is vibrant in personality and savvy at marketing on the internet. Such a study course can be conducted electronically by a private, non-credentialed individual, not in leadership of a synagogue or in a congregational setting, who personally lacks significant background or Bible training, and who has never undergone personal discipleship or mentorship from other qualified leaders. This is quite troubling when one considers that a person who holds no meaningful ordination is therefore accountable to no one.

In today's world of electronic communication, even the most unqualified person can nonetheless distinguish himself as a kind of "spiritual teacher" if he has a vibrant personality, communicates well through video, and has good skill level in multi-media marketing. From the perspective of Messianic Judaism, it is a somewhat dangerous scenario when a non-credentialed, untrained, un-mentored person with limited or no Bible training, and lacking accountability to messianic Jewish authority can hold himself out to be a "rabbi" and/or some kind of an authority as if speaking from within the messianic Jewish camp.

More specific to the issue at hand, we have seen this phenomenon with the teachers in the Hebrew Roots camp, who come out of nowhere to start large platforms, using the internet to self-promote, often calling themselves "messianic." Now the mesorah teaching is being promoted in much the same way. The divine oral Torah message is being promoted as if it is a messianic Jewish teaching, in spite of the fact that it violates the most basic belief of messianic Jews, as stated in our statement of faith, i.e. the authority of written Scripture. But the internet is open to anyone with a computer or mobile phone. This has great potential to confuse the public as to what Messianic Jews actually believe.

Accordingly, in recent years, through the use of social media and internet broadcasting – Facebook, YouTube, Websites, etc. – the mesorah teachers have promoted oral Torah as if part and parcel of normative messianic Jewish teaching. It isn't. In fact, that teaching which makes the writings of the rabbis on par with the Word of God is anathema to messianic Jewish teaching.

Conclusion:

Messianic Judaism is the living embodiment of God's end-time plan for the salvation and restoration of Israel. The oral traditions of rabbinic Judaism, though not divine in nature, nor given directly by God, clearly have an influence on all Jewish people, including Messianic Jews. Within Messianic Judaism many aspects of rabbinic Judaism are a positive influence. Some of it is embraced and practiced within our ranks. It is part of our culture and heritage as Jews.

This publication was not meant as a critique of rabbinic Judaism as a whole. It was aimed at exposing the central premise of rabbinic Judaism, which is the alleged divine nature of the Jewish oral tradition. Oral Torah is a myth, and the intent herein was to demonstrate that.

Moreover, as this is the day in which Jews are returning to faith in Messiah Yeshua, we maintain the hope and belief that Jewish people will continue to see how the oral Torah myth has kept our people in blindness toward the true identity of Messiah for generations. By exposing the oral Torah for what it truly is – a non-Torah – we are in sync with God's will, and His end-time plan for Israel's salvation is thereby advanced.

As Sha'ul said to Titus: "*Not paying attention to Judaic myths and commands of men who turn away from the truth.*"[126] Furthermore, as Sha'ul said to Timothy: "*Don't pay attention to myths and endless genealogies. These give rise to useless speculations rather than God's training which is in faithfulness.*"[127]

---

[126] Titus 1:14.
[127] 1 Tim. 1:4.

Instead of religious myths, it is time that our Jewish people put trust in Messiah. The messianic Jewish revival is at hand, and we have taken the lead in this regard. God's Spirit is given unto us to revive us. The gospel is returning to the one's who brought it to begin with – the Jewish people.

His Spirit also instructs us in the Word of God, given to mankind in writing, so that we might know the Lord, our Maker. It is that same Word of God, from Genesis to Revelation, which speaks plainly of Messiah who is the Alef and the Tav, the beginning and the end. His Kingdom is at hand. Yeshua HaMashiach, the same yesterday, today and forever.[128] Amen.

---

[128] Heb. 13:8.

Made in the USA
Columbia, SC
19 July 2019